CYCLES
of the
SOUL

CYCLES of the SOUL

Life, Death, and Beyond

CHANNELED TEACHINGS FROM JESUS

GINA LAKE

Endless Satsang Foundation

www.RadicalHappiness.com

Cover photo: © Agsandrew/DepositPhotos.com

ISBN: 979-8424704178

Copyright © 2022 by Gina Lake

All rights reserved. No part of this book may be used or reproduced by any means, graphic, electronic, or mechanical, including photocopying, recording, taping, or by any information storage retrieval system without the written permission of the publisher except in the case of brief quotations embodied in critical articles and reviews.

Contents

Introduction vii

CHAPTER 1   In the Beginning 1
The Soul—Guides, Angels, and Ascended Masters—Pre-life Planning—The Beginning of Life

CHAPTER 2   Free Will, Karma, and Challenges 23
Your Ego and You—Is There Free Will?—The Causes of Your Difficulties

CHAPTER 3   The Evolution of the Soul 45
The Earliest Lifetimes—The Stages of the Soul's Evolution—What to Do About Differences—How to Raise Your Vibration and Speed Up Your Evolution—Meditation—A Practice to Help Silence the Mind—A Prayer and a Practice—Practicing Kindness

CHAPTER 4   Karmic Justice and Healing Traumas 89
Near Deaths and Traumatic Deaths—Traumatic Accidents—Murder and Suicide—Unfortunate Love Affairs—Unfulfilled Potential—Slavery and Servitude—Mental Illness and Mental Disability—Imprisonment and Seclusion--Conclusion

CHAPTER 5   Death and Dying   163
How to Prepare for Your Death Throughout Life—Is Every Death God's Will?—What the Soul Gains from Death—What Happens Just Before Death—What Happens After Death—Ending One's Life

CONCLUSION   197

APPENDIX: The Astrological Signs   201

About the Author   223

Introduction

This book is somewhat of a departure from what I, Jesus the Christ, have been writing and speaking about through this channel, but it seems important to flesh out more fully the larger context in which your human life unfolds. As most of you reading this already know, at least intellectually, you are not human at all but spiritual beings who've taken on a human life—indeed, many human lifetimes—for a relatively brief time in your soul's existence as a means of exploration and spiritual advancement.

No matter how often you are told this, however, it bears repeating and further explanation because, to all but very advanced spiritual practitioners, it really seems that what you are is a human being. And yet, many of you have experienced, if only very briefly, that you are far vaster than this.

Human beings are but one form of humanoid life in your universe. There are endless universes in which human-like and other intelligent forms of life exist. This is not meant to make you feel small or unimportant, for you are anything but that. You are the created *and* the Creator! You are the Creator made manifest in human form—for the time being.

When you are released from your human form at death, you begin to remember and experience that you are much more than the human being you were in that lifetime. You remember that you lived many other human lifetimes, and most of you become more aware of what you were *before* those lifetimes. Even so, you won't realize your full magnificence and relationship to the Creator until your cycle of incarnations is complete.

Before taking on a human life, you existed as an energy being, as pure love and ecstatic beingness. And then you chose to experience being human. Once you did, you became embroiled in the cycle of lifetimes that hone and shape a human being and bring you back to your original state of love and peace—but with much more experience, compassion, and wisdom than you had before these incarnations. You chose to leave perfection for a state of imperfection and immeasurable challenges and growth. What courage! What a journey!

From these experiences as a human being, your soul gains immensely, far more than you can ever imagine, and not only your soul but the Godhead is enhanced by these experiences. All of creation evolves and all of creation evolves the Creator, and the Creator rejoices! This is what is going on. This is the bigger picture, the grand design that you are part of. So, let us explore this grand design further so that you also can celebrate and make the most of this precious human life.

Chapter 1

In the Beginning

The Soul

I will attempt to define the soul, but please understand that language is inadequate because your human form limits your ability to comprehend the greater mysteries of life. This is as it is meant to be. This limitation is part of the challenge of being a human being and what makes the experience of being human possible. You are intentionally cut off from your true nature, your divine nature, for the purpose of more fully exploring being human.

Being human puts limits on your divine nature. When you chose to become human, you chose to come into a limiting form, one that results in a narrow and distorted perspective that causes suffering. One of your challenges as a spiritual being in a human body is to learn to see beyond these mistaken perceptions to a truer one, to the extent that's possible as a human being. Nevertheless, not until you've completed your cycle of human lifetimes will you be able to see or understand life as you did before. While you are playing at being human, you are barred, for a relatively short time in your soul's evolution, from the heavenly existence you willingly chose to leave.

This limited and challenging perspective is *why* you chose to become human. The limitations are the point, not a mistake in the design or something that's personally your fault and certainly not a punishment. This is important to see. Your faults, failings, and limitations as a human being are in your design—in everyone's design—and you accepted this condition when you agreed to be human. These are not personal failings but grist for your spiritual mill. Every human being is saddled with essentially the same faults and limitations, although over the course of your many lifetimes, these lessen, since that's one of the purposes of your many lifetimes, as we will see.

Your soul is perfect and complete—always—before your human incarnations and after. Your soul is unharmed and unstained by any experience you might have during your sojourns on earth or elsewhere. *And* your soul is evolving as a result of these sojourns. Your soul is perfect *and* your soul is evolving, as is the Godhead. Every experience adds to your soul and to the Godhead.

From the standpoint of your soul, there is no experience you can have on earth or elsewhere that is bad or a mistake, although there are choices that lead to pain and suffering for oneself and others. The soul accepts and appreciates all experiences for the growth they provide. There is no judgment from the soul or any other being guiding your soul's evolution and no punishment as the result of any of your choices except the natural cause and effect of the Law of Karma, whose purpose is always to teach, not punish.

It is so important for you to understand that whatever challenges karma brings into your life are ones your soul agreed to take on. No one is forced into a life situation or circumstance that is not of one's soul's choosing. No one is limited or challenged in ways that the soul has not welcomed and designed for itself in conjunction with guides. When you're on the other side, in touch with your soul, you are very courageous and embrace the unique opportunity for growth the earth plane provides.

I should also add that there are other vastly different reincarnational systems that a soul might become involved in besides yours that provide very different experiences than your reincarnational system.

And, you might be interested in knowing that many reincarnating on earth have also reincarnated or will reincarnate elsewhere, in some other third dimensional, or physical, world during their human reincarnational cycle. So, by no means are all of your physical incarnations solely on earth.

Your soul also has the option to not be involved in any reincarnational system and remain free and unlimited. Angels are an example of this. However, most beings do choose to experience limitation and challenge at some point, because such experiences are interesting and stimulating. And if you are eternal, why *not* challenge yourself?

So, what is the soul? I will give you a simple definition: The soul is a spark of God. Why is this a good metaphor for the soul? Because a spark has all the qualities of the fire it came from. A spark isn't the totality of the fire it came from, but it can expand and have a life of its own. And regardless of what happens to it, a spark is still fire. Its essential nature never changes, even as it changes shape and transforms itself and that which it touches.

Like a spark, your soul is the same essence as God, not less than or different in any way. It just isn't the totality of God. So, when I say that you are God, I mean that you and every other soul are of the same essence as God, and that essence is love. Your true nature is love.

God, the Source, chose to expand itself by creating material and nonmaterial universes and by living inside those creations. This is accomplished by God sending sparks of itself—souls—into creation to explore, play, learn, love, and further create. Through their experiences, these souls accumulate knowledge, understanding, and even greater love, and evolve as entities in their own right, while simultaneously remaining unified with God, who is partaking in that experience as well.

The soul is so magnificent and multidimensional that it can enter into many different lifetimes at once. This is who you are. You are this magnificent, multidimensional being masquerading, for the time being, as a simple human being, all for the purpose of further expanding in love and every other divine quality.

Do you realize that there is no end to the experience of love? Love has many qualities, and the development of these qualities and the intensity of love is endless. This is what God gains through incarnation in human form and other experiences. God is expanded—and by this, I mean that God is expanded in love, knowledge, and wisdom, just as your soul is through your various incarnations.

Every experience you have is stored in your soul as not only a memory, but as knowledge and wisdom. And in each successive lifetime, you draw upon this accumulated knowledge and wisdom. This wisdom is given to you intuitively when needed by the nonphysical beings guiding you. Although you might not be aware of this when it happens, it's one of the ways the soul guides you throughout your lifetime. This explains why those who've lived more lifetimes are wiser and make better choices than younger souls.

As a result of its many lifetimes, this individualized aspect of your soul evolves in wisdom, love, and every other quality you consider admirable, such as patience, acceptance, responsibility, reliability, discrimination, perseverance, courage, fortitude, humility, empathy, compassion, generosity, kindness, rationality, fairmindedness, love, and so many others. Naming all that you gain from your incarnations is impossible, as language cannot capture this. Your individualized soul and your greater soul are enhanced in unimaginable ways.

Only once you're beyond the reincarnational cycle are you able to realize what you've gained. While in a body, you're often quite unaware of the miraculous process of evolution taking place within you. The density of the earth plane is so great that it's difficult to see the purpose of life and the beauty and perfection of life's workings.

It's difficult to feel grateful for the life you so gladly took on and with such passion and fervor! Most human beings are quite unaware of their soul and its involvement in their life. If they were, they would more easily rejoice in this gift of life. Through these writings, I hope to help you become more aware of this and of the servants of God, the nonphysical beings who guide your life, who are with you throughout.

Guides, Angels, and Ascended Masters

When a soul chooses to enter a cycle of reincarnation, on earth or otherwise, this is by no means done casually or without a lot of assistance from very wise beings whose job it is to oversee this entry, since this is a momentous decision for a soul. Certain beings have the specialized task of helping souls choose their life purpose, challenges, lessons, who they will incarnate with, and overall plan at the beginning of each lifetime. Other beings oversee the unfolding of each person's life during that lifetime, while others oversee the unfolding of humanity as a whole. Various names have been given to the many beings involved in the evolution of human beings and humanity in general, the most common being "guides," "angels," and "Ascended Masters." For clarity, I'll define these briefly.

"Guide" is a term used specifically for beings who guide a soul's evolution in a reincarnational system, usually a system they graduated from and gained a great deal of knowledge and understanding of. Being a guide is an art and takes a great deal of experience beyond simply graduating from the physical plane, that is, completing the cycle of reincarnation. Those who train to be guides go through a lengthy and rigorous training under the supervision of other more advanced guides. Thus, there are both what you might call master guides, or guides that guide and train other guides, and guides who have varying levels of expertise.

Although not all guides are equal in their abilities, all guides can be trusted to have your highest good as their goal, so although they are fallible, they are not the least bit corrupt or corruptible in terms of their character, love, and dedication toward those they serve. Guides can be trusted to be working on your behalf if not always correct in the guidance or information they give.

I mention this because many channels and psychics depend on their guides to give them information their clients ask for, and most of what these guides offer is helpful. And yet, guides don't know everything and they can make a mistake. So, please keep this in mind when consulting with psychics and channels. That said, most guides don't work alone or gather their information without help from other guides, which lessens the likelihood of mistakes.

Most people have three to five guides who work with them at any one time. One guide stays with you your entire lifetime and knows you completely and intimately and was probably with you in other lifetimes, while the others come and go depending on what's needed. When you undergo a big change or simply grow up or take on a new course of study or change your profession, some of your guides are likely to change.

More specialized guides that help with particular professions, talents, and life purposes will show up when needed and leave when no longer needed. Some people have pre-life agreements with certain guides or other beings to carry out specific tasks, such as writing a book, creating art, composing music, inventing something, or doing energy work or other types of healing.

The more influence a person has in the world, the more likely they are to have more than the usual number of guides. For instance, a president would have many guides, since the decisions made by him or her affect so many. However, a guide's influence is only as great as the person's receptivity. If those guides aren't listened to, it's as if that person has none. This is why electing or selecting only people of good character to be in powerful positions is especially important. People of good character obviously have some connection with their guides, while those divorced from their soul's guidance have only their egos to rely on, which is a dangerous situation.

Your guides guide you in many ways, but the primary ways are through your intuition and through inner nudges, joy, "ah-has," excitement, a sense of "yes" or "no," and other people. These ways may seem too subtle to be effective, but even souls who are less advanced find themselves responding to these cues without realizing it. Everyone follows such cues more than they realize, and becoming more aware of them will help speed up your evolution.

Through these cues, your guides are always speaking with you, suggesting things to do, directions to go in, and people and information to pay attention to. You are far from alone! You have an entire team of beings working with you whose sole task (no pun intended) is to help you learn and grow as your soul intended. They are working with you 24-7, so please know this, and that will help you become more aware of them.

Angels are beings who sometimes intervene in the affairs of humankind, acting as guides, healers, helpers, and messengers but who have never taken on a human life. They are an example of a being who has never been involved in a cycle of reincarnation, but there are others.

Angels operate more freely and have less defined roles than guides, moving in and out of human affairs as needed. They aren't assigned to any one person or group but go wherever they're needed. Angels are unconditionally loving toward humankind and dedicated servants, going about their business as requested by a higher order of beings, called archangels, who direct them in their tasks.

One of their main tasks is assisting the dying in transitioning, to whom they deliver messages of comfort and love. They're also often involved in preventing accidents and deaths that aren't part of someone's life plan and are frequently seen or felt by those they save. Such rare, seemingly miraculous interventions are deeply transformative for those who've had this experience, as are near-death experiences and other encounters with the supernatural.

Angels appear to those who are able to see them as having wings, not because they actually have wings but because human beings imagine that a celestial being would need wings to inhabit higher realms. Their wings also represent their swift and gentle movement and sudden arrival. Angels, who have no particular appearance, since they're made only of light, comply in their appearance with human expectations and also manifest this way to bring solace and comfort to humans.

Ascended Masters are beings who have gone beyond the cycle of reincarnation and advanced even further, beyond most guides, to being teachers and guides for all of humanity. Ascended Masters are not personal guides but guide the affairs on earth in a way that personal guides cannot and do not.

While personal guides help people fulfill their life purpose and learn their lessons, Ascended Masters are involved in a broader plan and design for all of humanity. Ascended Masters are orchestrating the plan for humanity, not for a single human being, although every individual's soul's plan affects this greater plan. Ascended Masters do become involved in guiding individuals at times, when their life purpose relates to humanity's evolution as a whole. For instance, I or other Ascended Masters might be involved with individuals or groups who are trying to bring about world peace or raise consciousness or teach spiritual principles or stabilize climate change.

And yet, I want to emphasize that I am available to all who call upon me, for I and other Ascended Masters are able to perform countless tasks at once and be anywhere and everywhere in the blink of an eye. So, please, dear ones, do call upon me for help, healing, and upliftment, and I will do my best to assist you. This is true of any of your guides, angels, and other beings who exist to serve you.

Yes, we exist to serve you. You are that important. It is our greatest joy to be of service to you and to all of creation. In this way, evolution is supported and enhanced, as those above assist and serve those below. This includes those above us, for we are not the highest in the hierarchy of celestial beings. In deepest gratitude to those who serve us, we joyfully serve you.

Pre-life Planning

Because every life is very important to the soul, it chooses the circumstances of each lifetime very carefully in a pre-life planning session with a group of beings, including the individual's lifetime guide, others skilled at this very specialized task, and the souls of those who will be important in the upcoming lifetime, including those who agree to be of help. Among other things, the soul chooses the location, gender, family, general appearance, challenges, lessons, life purpose, certain events and meetings, and most importantly, the time of birth.

Why is the time of birth so important? Anything born at a particular moment in time is imprinted with the energy of that unique moment. This is why astrology works and is shown to be helpful in understanding what people are like and why they behave the way they do, among other things. The planets and stars don't cause someone to behave a certain way. Rather, they reflect the unique energies of that moment, which are identical to the individual's imprinting. Astrology allows you to know what someone's imprinting is. By studying someone's birth chart, you get a peek into that person's personality, psychological issues, karma and other lessons, talents, challenges, and life purpose.

The astrology chart provides a lot of information about the imprinting, or programming, that the soul chose for the individual before life to implement the soul's lessons and life purpose. However, the chart doesn't determine or describe how the individual will use that programming. Free will is a reality, and once the individual is born, he or she will make choices, mostly in keeping with that programming, but not necessarily. Furthermore, there are a tremendous number of possible choices that can be made within that programming. So, the birth chart by no means determines how that life will turn out. But it does describe the personality, behavioral tendencies, drives, talents, psychological issues, lessons, karma, and life purpose that the soul is working with in a particular lifetime.

Before life, the soul sets out to learn certain lessons, overcome certain challenges, develop certain talents or improve in certain ways, overcome failings or karma, and accomplish a life purpose, which could simply be doing any of the things I just named. For instance, one's life purpose might be to learn to be more patient or more compassionate or to balance some karma or to develop a talent or to overcome some challenge. Or the life purpose could be about accomplishing something in the world: fighting for a cause, bringing in new ideas or creations, shaping government, changing how people do things, helping people heal, or serving in some other way. People tend to think of a life purpose as a career or something that might make a difference in the world, but more often than not, the life purpose has to do with personal or spiritual growth.

The life purpose is visible in a general way in the astrology chart. As the person matures, the life purpose often becomes clear because of the person's choices. People tend to find their way to their life purpose. Most people are doing it! The astrology chart represents innate drives that propel a person in a particular direction, and most people do go in that direction. You feel drawn to doing something, you're excited about learning something, someone offers you an opportunity to do something that interests you—all of these are ways the soul encourages you along a path that will fulfill your soul's lessons and goals.

This is why spiritual teachings so often encourage people to follow their joy and do what they love, because this is how you are guided to do what you came into life to do. You are pushed and pulled in the right direction with love, joy, excitement, opportunities, and people who help you. Life is not meant to be difficult. In spite of its challenges, there is much grace in life. And this is what is meant by grace. Grace is the hand of God, or of your soul, nudging you, supporting you, and encouraging you in a direction that will fulfill the goals you set in your pre-life planning session.

One of the most important things the astrology chart confers is a personality, which is achieved through the signs in the chart. Everyone has a number of different signs, not just a sun sign, so everyone's personality is quite complex. It's a mixture of many traits, some of them opposing, which create internal conflicts that will need to be resolved. Examples of these traits are stubbornness, boldness, friendliness, seriousness, passivity, confidence, playfulness, optimism, unconventionality, courageousness, and impulsiveness.

Because an understanding of your astrology chart is so important to understanding your personality and your soul's journey, lessons, and purpose, a summary about the signs is included in an Appendix at the end of this book. This Appendix was compiled by this channel many years ago.

Your astrology chart is your costume, or the role you are playing and how you appear to others for this lifetime. You need a personality, a costume, to operate in the world, and since you can't exchange your personality for another and your personality doesn't go away even after spiritual awakening or enlightenment, you have to work with the personality you've been given. This means you have to learn to express the positive side of the signs in your chart.

For example, if you were born a Cancer and you don't like being so sensitive, you can't be a Leo, who isn't sensitive, but you can learn to work with that sensitivity and use it to your advantage. That sensitivity is, no doubt, purposeful for you. Once one gains some mastery of this sign, the sensitivity of this sign is a gift and integral to being of help to others. Souls often choose Cancer lifetimes when their life purpose involves service to others, particularly to their emotional needs.

Each sign has both positive and negative traits, and the goal is to express the positive traits and not the negative ones. For instance, Cancers, who are naturally sensitive to the needs of others, need to learn to not be overwhelmed by their feelings or the feelings of others. And they need to be sensitive to their own needs and not give themselves away in their service to others.

Those who easily express the positive traits of their signs are either old souls or souls who've had many incarnations with those signs and gained mastery in expressing them. Young souls or souls who come into life with signs that their soul is unfamiliar with will have a harder time expressing the positive traits of those signs.

You often see this with twins, who have nearly identical charts but may be quite different. One may be an older soul who more easily expresses the positive side of the signs in that chart, while the other may be a younger soul who is less adept at expressing those signs or who is unfamiliar with certain signs. Soul age is a big factor in how the signs are expressed and how the chart is used in someone's life. Differences in soul age explain why two people with similar charts might express the signs in that chart very differently.

The information in the Appendix is worth taking a look at for more than just information about your personality. The astrology signs are the curriculum and means of learning for the soul. For example, Aries needs to learn patience and cooperation, and *every* human being also needs to learn this and will eventually over the course of many lifetimes. What each sign needs to learn is what every human being needs to learn at some point, and most souls require many, many lifetimes to learn each of the lessons of the twelve signs.

Every soul has many, many lifetimes in each sign, until the lessons of that sign are mastered. However, most souls have favorite signs that they choose again and again out of enjoyment and resonance, even after they've mastered those lessons. Your soul's journey through the various signs is quite unique!

The place of birth is also an extremely important choice for most souls and often reveals something about the life purpose and what the soul might be learning. Location plays a big role in shaping one's experiences, opportunities, and beliefs, including cultural and religious beliefs.

For instance, if a person is born in a war-torn country, then that, for whatever reason, is the right experience for that soul. It might be that the soul was warlike in another lifetime and needs to realize the devastating effect of war. Or it might be quite the opposite—that the soul, as a result of experiencing the devastation of war in a previous lifetime, is dedicated to helping those going through this experience or helping to establish or promote peace.

It's safe to say that whatever situation or circumstance you were born into, including mental or physical disabilities, abuse or neglect, or extreme poverty, was a deliberate choice on the part of your soul, for any number of reasons, some of which will not be able to be known by you.

This is also true of the family you were born into. Every soul chooses the family it's born into very carefully. Even so, souls sometimes change their mind, resulting in a miscarriage. This is just something that happens sometimes, although not the only reason for a miscarriage.

The process of incarnating is extremely intense for the soul, and some souls change their mind about coming into this very dense world once that density begins to be experienced by it. Going from a higher realm to this one feels like being squeezed into a very tiny, dark place after having been very free and blissful and unencumbered.

The family that's chosen nearly always has connections from previous lifetimes with the soul coming into that family. When that isn't the case, the child may feel a sense of disconnection or distance or a vague feeling that he or she doesn't belong and a longing for the more perfect home that was left behind. On the other hand, souls who have many or deep connections with one or more family members may be quite ecstatic about rejoining them—or trepidatious, as the soul anticipates similar difficulties or challenges that it's had in the past.

Because family members tend to reincarnate again and again with each other in different roles, family members tend to have strong connections with each other and possibly karma they're working out together. Even those with karma with each other are often very drawn to each other because the souls of those individuals really do hope to learn what they may not have learned in the past.

Karma is experienced as a magnetic attraction and cosmic glue that attracts and keeps people together, even under very difficult circumstances, until that karma is released. When karma is involved, why two people remain together is often somewhat of a mystery to those involved and those around them, for the deeper purpose of such a relationship is rarely understood by the two involved. Karma is often one of the forces at work in romantic attraction, but there are other reasons and purposes for people falling in love.

No matter how ugly or difficult a relationship might have been in the past, souls embrace such opportunities to work things out and grow. On the other side, souls see life on earth as a precious opportunity and look forward to the challenges. It's only once they are in a body that they realize, or remember, how very difficult it can be to be human, with its fears, desires, and other emotions.

Being a human on earth with the kind of ego and emotions that go with that is extremely challenging, which is exactly why souls are eager to come to earth. However, this being one of the more dense and difficult places a soul can choose to go to, souls don't always accomplish what they hope to. Karma isn't always released, and sometimes even more karma is accrued.

Nevertheless, when you are on the other side, even very difficult lifetimes seem worth it, since lifetimes on earth are experienced as very brief to the soul. From the perspective of your soul, each lifetime is over in a blink of the eye, and whatever pain was experienced doesn't linger. On the other side, things look and feel very different, and going through whatever it has gone through is more than worth it to the soul. Only when you're in the body does a lifetime seem lengthy and overwhelmingly difficult. Furthermore, when you are a magnificent, eternal being and you know you can't be harmed by anything you experience, only expanded, why wouldn't you challenge yourself this way? This is why the soul is willing to reincarnate again and again.

I can't emphasize enough that you are not victims of your circumstances or experiences on earth but willing creators and explorers. You may *feel* victimized, because that is the story the ego tells, but that's never the truth. Your soul either chooses or allows you to have the experiences you have for your growth and evolution. Your soul welcomes every experience, and if you can learn to do this too, then you are very far along, indeed, in your evolution. This type of acceptance and understanding doesn't develop until your last incarnations, when you begin to realize who you really are, at least to the extent that you can as a human being.

In your pre-life planning session, you also choose to come in with others who will help you fulfill your goals or just love you. Not all important relationships are karmic. Everyone has many people in their lives with whom they have made pre-life agreements to give love, friendship, and support or aid in some form. Many of your best and longest friendships are with souls with whom you have contracts and with whom you've had many lifetimes. Family members do often fill this role as well.

Most of the important opportunities and gifts in your life were arranged before life, and many of the lesser ones as well. Whenever you feel compelled to help someone and doing so uplifts you or brings you joy, there was probably a pre-life agreement. A magical feeling happens for both people when a pre-life agreement is fulfilled. This is another form of Grace in everyone's life. It's good to be aware of this and acknowledge this when it happens. You have more spiritual connections with other souls than you probably realize.

Gender is another considered choice by the soul, although not as important as some of the other choices, especially today when the roles for each gender are not as rigidly defined as they used to be. The soul considers the challenges and blessings of each gender and chooses a gender based on how it may or may not serve its goals. There is plenty of challenge in being either gender in your world!

Souls tend to favor one gender over another in their incarnations, and this is allowed as long as they have fulfilled a required number of lifetimes as the other gender. If a soul has had many lifetimes as a particular gender, especially many lifetimes in a row, then the next lifetime with the opposite gender can be challenging.

Some in this situation feel like they're supposed to be a boy when born a girl or vice versa. Homosexuality and confusion about one's gender identity can be the result of having had many lifetimes with one gender and few lifetimes or no recent lifetimes with the other gender. There are other reasons for gender identity issues as well, which I won't go into, since this is a complex subject.

Although there's nothing wrong with homosexuality, being attracted to the same sex can be a very big challenge for a soul in a culture where this isn't accepted. Those who are homosexual took this on as their challenge for various reasons, and for many, this issue is central to their life purpose.

Being someone who is persecuted for being different is a teaching opportunity for the collective, so that's one reason homosexuality was chosen by some. When numbers of souls come in with this same purpose, the culture is forced to reassess its beliefs and values, and that is certainly happening today.

An examination of the pre-life planning session wouldn't be complete if it didn't include a mention of choosing one's death and other critical events and life-changing moments. As for one's death, the timing of it is set before life as a probability that can change. Rather than one set date of death, most have several points at which the soul might choose to leave. As with much of life, the soul plays this somewhat by ear while making choices that will best serve the soul's lessons and life purpose and sometimes the collective.

Although most of your life is not preplanned or predestined, certain life-altering events, usually challenging ones, are preplanned. Examples of this are a near-death experience or a critical injury or illness or an unexpected death of someone very close to you, like a child or spouse. Another possibility is something less challenging: a sudden rise to fame or prominence, which has its own kind of challenges. The most dramatic events in a person's life are usually ones the soul chose before life to experience. Such an event might have a date assigned to it, or the soul might play the timing of it by ear, inserting it into the life when it can best serve.

The Beginning of Life

When does life begin? Does it begin with the soul entering the body or at the first sign of a heartbeat or at conception? Your world is struggling to answer this question. The answer to this is, perhaps, more important in your own minds than it is from the soul's perspective. I don't mean to sound cavalier about life, for life is immensely precious and many souls are eagerly awaiting incarnation. However, from the standpoint of the soul, when and where to incarnate is usually quite flexible, as every soul has many options. And the soul is not impatient about reincarnating and will wait as long as it needs to for the right opportunity and situation. Time is not exactly of the essence in other dimensions, since it doesn't exist at all!

So, when a soul loses an opportunity to reincarnate because of a choice on the part of the mother to not have a child, that free will choice is accepted, and the soul adjusts and makes another choice. Whether that choice to not have a child was the "right" choice for the mother's soul is another issue.

In any event, free will is respected without judgment or harm to either soul. As I said, the soul is very flexible, and as with any aspect of one's plan, if the person's choices go against that plan, that choice is respected and the soul adjusts or tries again to bring the person around to making the choice that was once rejected.

The soul has ways of being quite persuasive when a particular choice is important to the plan. It doesn't take no for an answer if a yes is critical to the plan. It will find another way to bring something about if need be. Sometimes it does this by blocking the person from moving forward in the direction he or she is choosing, and other times, it does this by making the choice it wants the person to make irresistible. But many of the choices you make are just fine with the soul, and it goes along with what you are choosing to create, as it can use many different situations for its growth.

The soul doesn't fully and permanently enter the body until birth, at which point the soul is said to be born and its life begins. It is the soul that breathes the body at birth, for there would be no life and no breath without the soul.

The incoming soul and the souls of the mother and family members agree sometime during gestation to be together and stick to that agreement. That agreement might even be made before conception if there are many past-life connections and a strong need to come into that family. After that agreement is made, the soul stays close to the fetus and mother and sometimes joins with the fetus but not fully and permanently until birth.

Nevertheless, some souls slide in at the last minute, if the assigned soul suddenly changes its mind and backs out. There is no shortage of souls looking to incarnate, and many of them can benefit from any number of parents and situations.

Chapter 2

Free Will, Karma, and Challenges

The Ego and You

Once you are in the body and take your first breath, you are alive—and you are human! What an adventure! You don't always feel this way initially. Being born is traumatic for most souls. There was comfort in the womb, and now there are bright lights, loud noises, people coming and going, and all of it is unfamiliar. The more difficult the birth was, the more the baby is affected by that experience, but every birth is difficult for every soul. It's an enormous shock to come from a realm of light and love into the density of this plane.

What I mean by density is that the earth plane vibrates at a much lower rate than the nonphysical dimensions. What this means is that the sense of separation from Source is greater. You feel separate and alone, disconnected, in a way you never did in the higher dimensions. No matter how much love you receive when you enter the world, it can't begin to match the love you felt where you came from.

When you come into a body, everything feels different. Everything *is* different. And yet, you still remember what it was like where you came from. You remember this for quite a while as a baby and somewhat into childhood, until that memory fades and you're left primarily with your ego's perceptions of the world.

The increasing sense of separation as you grow up is part of the process of incarnation, and some souls take the loss of this sense of connection with Home very hard, while others seem to rejoice in returning to this world. Much depends on how many lifetimes you've had on earth. The more lifetimes you've had on earth, the more easily you accept the conditions on earth and are able to deal with them.

This makes sense. If you were an explorer in a strange world, your first forays in that world would feel stressful and challenging, but once you're accustomed to a place, it begins to feel like home. The same thing happens to souls. The oldest souls learn to love earth and often come back even when they don't have to, to serve. This is what I did when I took on the lifetime you are so familiar with.

As you grow up, you acquire a sense of yourself as separate from your mother, other family members, and your surroundings. You develop an ego. This is a necessary development, which happens very early. You need an ego to operate in the world; you need a sense of "I." However, the egoic programming that gives you this sense of "I" also programs you with fear and a sense of lack, of not being good enough or having enough, and also with an unceasing desire for more and better, as the ego defines that.

The egoic programming is very limiting and negative, which is why life on earth seems so difficult. *It* is the cause of suffering, not so much what happens to you. You are programmed with an ego, a voice in your head, that tells you scary and untrue stories about yourself and life. You are programmed to believe that you are more limited than you are and in imminent danger. If those around you also give you this message, which they can't help but do to some extent because of their own egos, then you feel all the more limited, fearful, and lacking. And those who feel this way often lash out at others in hurtful ways. In this way, life on earth becomes as the ego believes it to be, and the cycle of suffering continues. This is the human condition.

The ego is what makes the earth plane so dense. It was designed to do this for the challenge this provides. This world is one of the more challenging worlds, and that is no mistake. There are other third dimensional planets with human-like beings who have egoic programming that isn't nearly as limiting or negative. The ego is programming, and that programming is unique everywhere there's an ego. The Creator enjoys creating unique worlds and experiencing them.

This egoic programming is also responsible for your negative feelings: your fear, hatred, anger, resentment, jealousy, shame, envy, self-pity, and sadness. Your particular emotional makeup is also unique to earth. Everyone who comes here is learning about this form of ego and the emotions it generates. Everyone is learning to overcome the limitations and negative emotions produced by their egoic programming.

First, as a child, you develop an ego, and then as you mature, you learn to control your ego and its negativity. Then later in your spiritual evolution, you learn to transcend the ego. That is the purpose of my teachings, to help free you—save you, if you will—from the negativity of your egoic programming by teaching you the truth about life. I have no other real means of saving you. You must save yourselves by discovering the truth.

Until you've seen that your ego is detrimental programming, you believe that you *are* what the ego tells you that you are. You believe the voice in your head, which reflects this programming. Yes, this voice, that most people think of as their own thoughts and beliefs—their personal "truth"—is the voice of the ego or the voice of conditioning you've received from parents and others—the voice of *their* egos. It isn't that some of this conditioning isn't useful—some of it is—but much of it isn't useful and only pretends to be. I'm here to help you see this and break free of this programming.

The truth is that you are not your programming; you are what is *aware* of the voice in your head. You are aware of this now that I've told you this, or perhaps you've heard this teaching before. Regardless, right now, you're aware that you have a voice in your head that isn't your true voice and isn't who you are but merely programming. If this is the first time you've heard this, then this is probably a shock. But realizing this is the first step in cracking the door open to your freedom, to becoming free of this limiting and untrue programming.

Who is it that needs to be free or who becomes free? This is a great mystery, isn't it? Who are you really? You are what is conscious and aware of your life. When you came into this life and took your first breath, you became conscious, and that which is conscious is who you are. You are not what you think about yourself or what others think or say about you. That's the false self, what the programming causes you to believe about yourself. The true self is what is conscious and aware. It is what incarnated. It is the spark of your greater soul that chose to come here and have this limiting and challenging experience on earth in order to grow in wisdom and love.

Until you become aware of who you really are, your ego, through the voice in your head, runs your life most of the time. This is the situation you undoubtedly found yourself in, in most of your previous lifetimes. You weren't aware of who you really are until a certain point in your evolution, such as now, when you became aware of this.

It takes hundreds, even thousands, of lifetimes to get to this place in one's evolution when you are aware of the programming that caused you to believe that you were something other than what you are. What a momentous lifetime it is when this dawns! You are finally free to choose from a higher will, no longer tossed to and fro by the ego's will. Then, your soul's will, otherwise known as Thy will, begins to operate more naturally through you, and you become an instrument of Grace rather than a creator of karma.

Once your true nature is realized, life is much easier and feels much better. No longer are you at the mercy of negative emotions and the resulting poor choices. Some of you, out of great courageousness and a desire to serve, will still choose to experience big challenges. But even then, because of your connection with your soul, you'll have the strength to overcome those challenges and come out wiser, stronger, and more compassionate.

Is There Free Will?

The choices you make before life and the choices you make during your life are very important to the soul. They determine your experience of each lifetime and drive and shape your evolution. The soul is all about having experiences and learning, and the way for a soul to have unique, educational, and interesting experiences is to allow for free will, for what would be the point of living out a predestined life?

The fun is in exploring the unknown, and free will makes it possible for life to be an unfolding mystery, one that offers not only challenges but interesting and surprising turns: What will happen next? What if I try this or do that? Even your soul doesn't know exactly how your life will turn out, thanks to free will. Through free will, the soul grows, expands, and becomes wiser and more loving. And it has fun! The soul loves even the challenges.

So, I'd like to say more about this rather complex subject of free will. Is there free will or not? Yes! The answer is that yes there is and no there isn't. Both are true. Let me explain.

You are definitely free to choose what to have for breakfast, for instance, right? You can choose yogurt or oatmeal or something else. However, the options you consider and the choices you make around this are determined by your habits, preferences, what's considered breakfast food, what your body is able to tolerate, beliefs about what's good for you and what you should eat, and unconscious forces.

So, how free is your free will when your choices are circumscribed by these things—by conditioning and circumstances? So, yes, you have free will, but your choices are limited and shaped and determined by many factors.

There also are many things that have already been set by your soul, which you're no longer free to choose: You aren't free to choose what gender or race you are, how tall you are, or your general appearance. You aren't free to choose your children or a different family or a different past. You aren't free to choose how events will unfold or what will happen in the future. You aren't even as free as you may think to choose your spouse, lovers, or friends, as many of these relationships are also arranged in your pre-life planning session.

Once you're in the body, there are many more things you aren't free to choose than what you are free to choose. There's much more in life that just happens to you beyond your control than what you're able to control with your free will. It turns out that your will is a minor factor in the scheme of things and not all that free but shaped by many forces.

However, there is one very important thing that you are free to choose, which will determine your level of happiness, your experience of life, and how quickly you progress in your evolution, and that's your attitude toward your experience: You are free to choose to be happy about something or upset, to be angry, sad, or resentful or to accept something.

Although you aren't in control of much of what you experience, you *can* choose your inner climate, or attitude toward your experiences. And you can choose beliefs that will help you be happy and accepting of life. This is one of the most important lessons in life! This is what life is really about, not getting what you want or making your life turn out a certain way, but learning to be happy and at peace. From there, the most important thing of all flows: love.

You can always choose to be happy, grateful, accepting, at peace, and loving. *Always.* Maybe you won't feel happy or grateful for a particular experience, but your overall state can be one of happiness and gratitude if you focus on the things in your life that make you happy and grateful and not on the things that don't. The ego does the opposite of this. In many respects, your soul's evolution depends on learning to do the opposite of what your ego would do.

However, unless you learn to become *aware* of your thoughts and feelings and make an effort to choose against the programming, your thoughts and feelings will control you, not the other way around. Your free will won't be free to choose against the conditioning. Awareness of your thoughts and feelings is key.

Where does this awareness come from? It obviously doesn't come from the ego. Awareness is a quality of your divine nature. When the Divine begins waking up in you, it does this by making you more aware of the programming, often through spiritual teachers or teachings. You become more aware of your thoughts and the feelings that stem from them rather than being lost in them and at the mercy of them.

Once a certain amount of awareness has awakened within you, you start making different choices—better choices, ones more aligned with peace, joy, and love. But before this awareness has developed, people are at the effects of their programming. They have a very limited ability to choose. They choose within their programming, on the basis of their preferences, habits, egoic desires and fears, what they've been taught, what they've learned or concluded, and unconscious factors and drives, including astrological tendencies. So, how free is that will? If your programming is determining your choices, can we say that you are freely choosing?

So, you see, the small will—the will of the ego and choices determined by one's conditioning and astrology—is not that free. It appears free, in that you can choose yogurt or oatmeal, for instance. You can even choose to go to law school instead of majoring in English, which is a much more important choice than what you have for breakfast. But even bigger choices are determined to a large extent by your astrological tendencies and, importantly, your soul's plan, which is also a type of programming.

In fact, your life is being continually shaped by a larger will—by Thy will, or your soul's intentions. So, even if you choose to go to law school, if you're meant to be a writer, you'll be steered by the hand of Grace away from law into a more appropriate course of study.

You are allowed to follow the small will only as long as it doesn't interfere with Thy will, with your soul's plan. Thy will always trumps the small will. Often the small will doesn't interfere, but when it does, life finds a way to stop you from going in the direction your small will is taking you and opens up opportunities in the direction of what your soul needs and wants to experience.

Opportunities and blocks are the means the soul uses to steer your life and co-create with you. It works with you by either allowing you to go after what your ego wants or preventing you from doing this. Quite often, what your ego wants isn't a problem for the soul, and it works with that or works around that. And quite often, you happily choose to follow your divine self's drives and passions, which are given to you intuitively.

As you progress spiritually, Thy will is increasingly at the helm. Thy will *becomes* your will, as you surrender the ego's will to what's coming out of the flow and to the guidance you're being given intuitively. This takes practice, but by the end of your incarnations, living this way is natural and easy.

Awareness of your thoughts and feelings is what allows divine will to come forward and take the helm. Its development can be hastened through spiritual practices, particularly meditation. This development is key to true freedom, which ironically is freedom to be nobody special but to be your divine self, the same consciousness that abides in everyone.

When Thy will is the will that you are following, can we even speak about it as free will, when it feels more like no will and no need for a will? When the small will is surrendered, all that's left is Thy will, which doesn't belong to you at all. When there is no you (no false self, no egoic self) with a will, can we even call what remains free will?

Thy will becomes simply whatever is true to do in any moment. What you do becomes a choiceless choice. Your soul is running the show now. There is no longer a sense of having a false self that would argue or prefer or choose anything but the natural unfolding that's already occurring of which you are a part. When you are one with All That Is, your will is the same as whatever's already happening.

The Causes of Your Difficulties

There are a number of reasons people experience difficulties in life, not the least of which is that it would be impossible to live in a physical body with the physical laws that exist and not have difficulties. Physical bodies get hurt, they break down, they age, and they die. To the ego, all these things are felt to be a problem, since the ego doesn't like that these things occur.

The ego puts a negative spin on such things, a story, which makes you feel bad about these very normal and natural occurrences: "That shouldn't have happened," "I look awful," "getting old is terrible," "death is frightening." These are things that happen to everyone, that no one escapes. Why make yourself miserable about them? This is just what human beings do because they have an irrational ego that does this. Without the ego, there would be simple acceptance of these facts of life and much less suffering.

So, that's the first reason you experience difficulties: You have an ego that turns natural occurrences into a problem, a difficulty. Learning not to do this is one of the most important lessons of your human evolution. This is no small task and takes hundreds, if not thousands, of lifetimes before one sees that this is what's going on and that there's no problem with so many of the things that happen in life. They are natural, normal, and not a problem.

Why does it take so long to see this? Because it's meant to take long. You have lots of other lessons to learn as an ego before you're ready to see the truth and transcend the ego. You aren't programmed to realize the truth about life and the human condition until you have a certain mastery of the basic lessons of being human. These are the lessons, as I said, of the twelve astrology signs. You are meant to be fully human and have the experiences your ego creates. The ego is the grist for your spiritual mill. You must experience being this limited, fearful self for many, many lifetimes until you are ready to awaken.

This might sound cruel or unfair, so I'll remind you that if you're reading this, you have the most difficult lessons behind you, as you're obviously ready to awaken to the Truth. And, I'll remind you that your soul gladly chose all those challenges and is leaping for joy at this momentous moment in your incarnations when you are delving into the Truth, healing your misunderstandings, and striving to become the loving being you've always been at your core.

This waking up process is slow but steady, and you must be patient with all of it: with the time it takes, with the mysterious and unknowable experience that it is, and with others who aren't as advanced as you are in your understanding—with those who are still very stuck in the egoic state of consciousness.

For them, that is the right experience for the time being, and you don't need to do anything about that unless they want your help with their spiritual growth, which certainly happens. You are each other's teachers, and being an awakener of others and a spreader of the Truth is one of the roles you play in your later lifetimes.

One of the main reasons people experience difficulties, other than the tendency of the ego to spin everything into a problem, is that people make poor choices and they made poor choices in other lifetimes, leading to karma in the current one.

The fact that you have free will is a mixed blessing. The soul evolves as a result of free will, so that is the blessing. However, the ability to choose your own course and learn from those choices also leads to suffering along the way.

Most difficulties and emotional pain indicate that some choice you made to do or say or believe something was not a good choice for you. That choice may be going against your soul's plan or against love or simply a choice to believe something that isn't true.

The soul guides you to fulfill your soul's plan by putting difficulties in your path when necessary along with opportunities. And the soul teaches you to love through negative and positive feedback from others and by experiencing the suffering created by your own negative beliefs and emotions. The soul shows you what choices don't work through negative feedback and which ones do work through positive feedback.

When things don't work out as you hoped or when people are unkind to you, it's *sometimes* because you brought that upon yourself, although not always. Sometimes people respond badly for no reason, and sometimes difficulties just happen because people have free will and don't always choose wisely. Some of your difficulties are due to other people behaving badly because of their poor choices and have nothing to do with you.

It can be difficult to tell the difference between these two things. Is life or are people getting in your way for your own good, or are they out of alignment with *their* plans and, therefore, causing problems with the unfolding of your plan.

You may never know the answer to such questions, and you have to accept that.

The soul is constantly making course corrections in response to the free-will choices of others, which it can't always control. Everyone has free will, and sometimes others are listening to their soul's guidance and sometimes they aren't. Life isn't always going to go according to your soul's plan. Your soul knows this and is very flexible and adaptable, and so must you be.

Life is messy, but that makes life interesting. If you can learn to see life this way rather than as a problem, you can be happy in spite of any situation or outcome. You aren't in control of how life is unfolding but a mere actor in this immense drama playing out on this plane. Your own will and choices affect everything but so do other people's. That makes life unpredictable — and that's interesting and fun!

You are here to learn and you are also here to enjoy yourself. So, it's important that you learn to love life. Love is the basic lesson in life, which includes learning to love life.

The way to love life is to accept that life is the way it is and to accept whatever happens, since it happened. This is the only sensible thing to do. Railing against life only makes you miserable. However, seeing this takes a great deal of rationality, which isn't available to human beings until much later in their evolution. Before that, they're led mostly by the irrational ego, and life doesn't make sense to the ego.

Throughout your incarnations you are learning the lesson of love. This means not only being loving to others, but to yourself. To be loving to yourself means making choices that don't make you suffer. This includes making conscious choices about what you believe, since mistaken beliefs are behind every unpleasant emotion and harmful act.

When you choose to accept whatever is happening, you're loving yourself by choosing a path of no suffering. And, in doing so, you're also choosing to love life. Yes, this is a choice, perhaps not an easy one, but the more you choose to love and accept life, the easier life becomes.

So, another thing that creates difficulties, besides the difficulties others knowingly or unknowingly create for you through their choices, is making choices that are not aligned with your soul's plan or that are harmful or hurtful to others and that might even incur karma.

It isn't easy to make choices from a higher, deeper place—from your soul. It's much easier to let your ego make choices without bringing any awareness to what you're choosing. The ego is your default, but the more you recognize what it's choosing and the negative consequences of those choices, the more power you have to override the ego's will and make a truly free-will choice, one that is your soul's choice.

As I said earlier, the ego's choices are not really very free. Most of them are knee-jerk, automatic responses to life that don't consider the deeper consequences of those choices. For instance, you say something unkind to someone because that's what comes out of your mouth—you just feel like saying it, so you do—and that has long-lasting consequences for your relationship.

In the egoic state of consciousness, there's very little space between when a thought arises and when it's bought into and expressed. In the egoic state of consciousness, there's no questioning of your thoughts—they're yours, after all! Or are they?

The beauty of meditation is that it allows for a space—the briefest of seconds—between a thought arising and believing it or expressing it. In that gap, is freedom—true freedom—not freedom to express whatever you want, whatever your ego wants, but freedom to *not* express something.

This freedom to not be at the mercy of your thoughts but to be able to consciously choose what you'll put out into the world is the freedom to be who you really are. Finally, you can express your soul in the world instead of the ego. Finally, you are free to be you—the real you!

Not being free in this way is a problem for the world because expressing the ego is why this world is so very difficult. It's not that life on this material plane is so very difficult, but the ego makes it so. Your conditioning, thoughts, and beliefs, which resist the way things are and tell stories that make you unhappy, make it so.

Most of what you think and believe comes from the ego and from what you've been taught by other egos. These thoughts make you feel angry, unhappy, discontent, sad, confused, and every other emotion you struggle with. This is your grist for the mill, but there comes a time for this cycle of suffering to be overcome, and that time, for many of you, is now.

Beliefs cause all the suffering in the world, only because people hold so many false beliefs, ones not aligned with love. If your beliefs were different, more aligned with Truth, there would be little suffering. Mistaken beliefs cause negative feelings, and these feelings cause harmful actions and similar responses from others.

This is how karma is created: You believe something that isn't true, then your certainty about that generates strong feelings, and those strong feelings justify hurtful and harmful behavior toward others. If you weren't so sure of your beliefs and your feelings weren't so strong, you wouldn't feel justified in behaving in such ways. You would stop yourself, because deep down you do know better. Even very young souls have goodness at their core and only harm others out of fear and desperation.

Where does fear come from? It lies latent in human beings, like a beast within you that needs just a little poke to get going. That poke comes from entertaining thoughts that stoke fear, and those thoughts lead to more feelings, until holding back your words or actions becomes nearly impossible.

Who is responsible for these thoughts and feelings? You're not responsible for having an ego; it's part of your software. And you're not responsible for the thoughts produced by this software, this programming. However, you *are* responsible for any feelings you experience, because they are the result of giving your attention to the thoughts produced by the programming.

You are responsible for choosing to feed any mistaken thoughts that arise in your mind. It is a choice to do this, although it may not seem like one. When you're a younger soul, there isn't much choice around this, which is why a great deal of karma is created in your earlier lifetimes. But you learn from these lifetimes and become more able to dismiss such thoughts rather than entertain them. By your later lifetimes, you're much less likely to act out your feelings in detrimental ways and more adept at not creating problems and karma. However, you might still have karma that needs balancing from earlier lifetimes, and the ego can still cause problems.

Most of the biggest challenges people experience in their lives are karmic. These challenges were created by poor choices, and a person will experience difficulties related to these poor choices until he or she learns to make different choices. Most karmic lessons and more general ones are about learning to behave differently in relationship to others, in a nutshell: learning to make the loving choice.

Karma around some actions may take lifetimes to balance and is balanced in one or more of the following ways: by role reversal, by benefiting the one you harmed in some way, or by benefitting someone else or a particular group of people in place of the one you harmed. A karmic debt doesn't always have to be repaid directly to the one harmed; it can often be repaid through others.

Balancing karma is tricky, and sometimes more karma is created in the process. These situations must be chosen very carefully by the souls of those involved. Even with a role reversal, there's no guarantee that karma will be released when two people are brought together again. People who are meeting again to release karma can become embroiled in a situation similar to the one they were in, in the past and not change. Because there is free will, people don't always behave as their souls had planned or hoped.

What makes these relationships particularly difficult when they don't go as planned is that, with karma, some karmic "glue" is usually involved, which is intended to bind individuals together to work out their karma. This "glue" remains even if the situation is failing or has failed to release the karma. For instance, there might be children involved that keep a couple together or other family or business ties that cause those individuals to be thrown together or stay together against their desires. Sometimes, all that results is a deeper entrenchment of the emotional patterns that got them into trouble in the first place.

This information about karma is meant to be helpful, not heap more suffering on an already difficult situation. It's important to remember that you do have free will, and if your relationship is toxic and not working, make another choice. You are free to leave a relationship that seems karmic. The soul will try again to balance the karma some other way. There is no shame in this; this happens all the time. Sometimes, relationships or situations must be left because remaining in them only brings out the worst in people.

It's also important not to feel victimized by such difficult relationships or to assume that you're a terrible person because you have karma to balance. For one thing, you can't know this for sure. But what's most important to understand is that nearly everyone is dealing with balancing karma. It can be no other way. This is how the soul learns and evolves.

Your ego might feel ashamed or upset about the idea that you might still have karma to balance, but karma is just another fact of life, just something more the ego has to accept about life. You are flawed, everyone is flawed, and evolution progresses on the basis of making mistakes and trying again to do better. That's all karma is, really. Your soul is trying to do better than it did under previous circumstances. Like an actor taking another take: "Try again this time to be a little more understanding, patient, and kind, and see what happens."

Another reason for your difficulties is that accidents *do* happen. The soul isn't always able to protect someone from an accident. Unexpected things happen, and sometimes people make unanticipated choices that result in an accident. If a soul or souls aren't meant to experience that kind of difficulty, the soul or souls can usually affect the outcome of an accident, at least somewhat, and lessen the harm, but not always. People don't always hear or heed the inner guidance they're receiving even when it's a distinct voice in their head, or things may happen so quickly that intervention isn't possible.

Some accidents are part of your soul's plan, but when they aren't, they can throw off the soul's plan, which will need to adjust. Accidents, like the mistakes and mistaken choices that likely caused them, are part of life, and the soul will find a way to make the best of even that experience.

So far, I've mentioned several reasons why you may experience difficulties or problems. They are:

❖ Your ego frames everything as a problem, even things that aren't problems;

❖ You have free will and make poor choices based on faulty beliefs and the negative feelings that flow from them;

❖ You behave badly toward others, and they respond in kind;

❖ Other people cause problems for you because of their poor choices, which have nothing to do with you;

❖ You are balancing karma; and

❖ Accidents happen that are not part of your soul's plan.

Another very important reason you may experience difficulties is that your soul, out of courageousness and not necessity, chose before life to take something on as a challenge. This is often the case with life-shaping challenges, such as disabilities or abusive situations, although these could also be karmic.

In addition, the soul sometimes takes on a challenge in the midst of life that wasn't part of the pre-life plan. This might be done because the habit patterns or course of life needs to be shaken up to get the individual back on track with the soul's plan. Or, it might be done because a situation, which wasn't foreseen before life, is felt to be optimum for a particular lesson. The soul will often take advantage of unexpected opportunities to learn.

It's very important not to judge others for their difficulties, disabilities, or other challenges. Such challenges are not necessarily the result of karma but may have been chosen by an older soul for various reasons. It's not your place to judge or make assumptions about why someone is having a particular experience. This is not something you can know, and it's best to be humble enough to admit this. That humility will allow your Heart to stay open to them.

The ego is out for itself, so it will use information about karma to absolve itself of the responsibility of having to care for or help those who are disadvantaged or undergoing difficulties. But that judgmental, cold-hearted attitude will only likely lead to a lesson in compassion and empathy, possibly a role reversal in another lifetime. One way or another, life will humble the ego, because the purpose of life is to shine light on the ego's destructiveness, and the soul will design lessons to do just that.

The antidote to judging is to realize that you are your brother's keeper, for the tables have been or will be turned sometime, because that's how life works. "Do unto others as you would have them do unto you" is the most basic and most essential lesson that humanity is learning. It is the lesson of love.

Challenges the soul chooses before life or in the midst of life tend to be less difficult to handle than karmic lessons or the difficulties that young souls experience by virtue of being young. Souls who take on a significant challenge for their growth do so because they, in consultation with their guides, believe they're strong enough to use that challenge for their benefit or because they want to accelerate their evolution.

The soul doesn't set anyone up for failure by making certain choices, but sometimes a soul takes on more than the individual can handle. The complexity or difficulty of some challenges once one is in the body sometimes prove to be too much for the individual, in which case the soul will choose more cautiously next time.

Regardless of the reason for or cause of a difficulty, the soul can and does learn from it, even from an accident. Something is always learned, if not the intended lesson. Unfortunately, sometimes people come to wrong conclusions in reaction to their difficulties—they learn the wrong thing.

They might blame others or feel victimized or feel that they're at fault when they aren't. These incorrect conclusions cause a great deal of suffering, leaving people feeling regretful, angry, vengeful, self-pitying, hateful, jealous, envious, ashamed, or guilty when they don't need to. Their beliefs and stories about their experience make them feel terrible.

Many also, unfortunately, believe that they *should* feel terrible if something bad happened or they made a mistake, so they punish themselves again and again with self-hatred, regret, guilt, and shame. This serves no purpose. Doing this to yourself or retaliating against others is the opposite of learning what you're meant to learn in difficult times.

You're meant to overcome such feelings through understanding, compassion, acceptance, and forgiveness for yourself and others. This is the answer to life's difficulties. This is all that's asked of you. Accept that you or another made a mistake, have compassion for yourself or another, forgive yourself or another, and do your best not to repeat the mistake.

The problem with blame, hatred, and every other negative feeling, no matter how justified these feelings may seem, is that they keep you tied to the past. They make you a prisoner to an experience that's over and done with. They keep you stuck in the egoic state of consciousness, stuck in a state of suffering, where growth and learning aren't possible. This does no one any good and is a waste of a beautiful life. It sometimes takes a lifetime or more of living in such a state before a person is able to move beyond this. Such is the human condition.

Growth and learning are all about leaving this state of consciousness behind and living from another, freer and more loving state of consciousness: your divine nature. This is your birthright, and by the end of your many incarnations, you know exactly what that looks like. This is the reward of all your lifetimes. Finally, you get to be at peace. Finally, you love life and see it as the gift that it is.

In this examination of the causes of your difficulties, I hope it is apparent that, as important as your thoughts and beliefs are in creating your experience of reality, your thoughts and beliefs are by no means the only thing responsible for your experience of life, including your difficulties. If the statement "you create your reality" includes the "you" that is your soul, then this statement becomes truer. But "you," the egoic self, the false self, is by no means the only shaper of your reality or reality in general.

Your free will is an important player, but your soul, or Thy will, is the ultimate arbiter of what happens, and other people's free wills have a hand in this as well. You co-create your reality with all of life, with every soul and every other person's free will. Life is a beautiful, mysterious, messy, unpredictable, complex intermingling of countless forces, and everyone, including everyone's soul, is playing it by ear.

Chapter 3

The Evolution of the Soul

Every soul experiences hundreds, if not thousands, of incarnations and advances through various lessons and stages. In the earliest lifetimes, the lessons pertain primarily to physical survival and gaining basic skills. Once these are sufficiently mastered, the soul's focus turns to emotional development and learning to build bonds with others. Next, the focus is on ego development: learning to be independent, achieving one's goals, and developing certain talents. Following that stage, the emphasis becomes mental pursuits, psychological growth, the further honing of specific skills and talents, and contributing to society and the well-being of others. The final stage of evolution is about spiritual development, further development of the intellect and one's skills and talents, and refining one's ability to serve, as one's true nature comes forward and is expressed more.

The Earliest Incarnations

When the soul enters a human body for the very first time, that soul is already perfect, immaculate, and whole. It is incarnating not because it needs to for any reason but because it wants the particular experience of being a human being. It wants the challenge of the limitation and distorted perceptions inherent in being human. It chooses to forget its magnificence, where it came from, and all it knew before to come into the human form as a blank slate, with only the programming it's given that allows it to function.

This programming is the ego, which is a survival mechanism, but only in the most primitive sense. The ego, although necessary, is actually maladaptive for living in a complex society because the ego is selfish and poor at cooperating and sharing, which are essential for communities and societies to survive. Nevertheless, the ego is a necessary and permanent feature because it provides the sense of individuality and separation from Oneness needed to pretend, for the time being, that you are a human being.

The incoming soul also has astrological programming that provides certain drives, behavioral tendencies, and a personality style. As a result of that programming and genetics, every human being, like every snowflake, is unique and programmed in such a way as to ensure that uniqueness, for why would God create duplicate experiences?

Newborn souls have so much to learn! They don't come in knowing how to be human or with the wisdom of their later incarnations. They don't even know how to love as a human being. Their essence, like all souls, is love, but the density of this plane is such that their true nature is veiled from them. Consequently, they have to learn to love, which is what this earth-school is all about.

The degree of love that the youngest souls are capable of feeling is very limited. What love and joy they do experience is closer to appreciation than love as most people know it. However, that can turn to anger and hate very quickly if their protectors fail to shield them or abdicate this responsibility.

In addition to learning to love, newborn souls have to begin to learn all the other lessons of being human, as described by the astrological signs. Learning these lessons will take the length of all their incarnations. These are lessons such as patience, perseverance, humility, courage, discrimination, practicality, tolerance, caution, responsibility, self-direction, independence, empathy, cooperation, and assertiveness, to name a few. Such qualities are lacking in the newborn soul and are only developed over many, many lifetimes as a result of training, making mistakes, and encountering challenges.

Newborn souls are also learning how to deal with their emotions in ways that don't make life more difficult. This is a lesson that continues throughout most of a soul's lifetimes, as emotional mastery is rarely attained until the soul's later lifetimes, and imperfectly even then.

Fear is the newborn and very young soul's overriding emotion. This is because fear is the ego's default emotion, and in the early lifetimes, the ego is running the show. When very young souls are confronted or feel threatened, they either withdraw or lash out angrily or even violently. Their anger is automatic, uncontrolled, and primitively expressed.

Newborn and very young souls also often use fear to intimidate or manipulate others into doing their bidding, since they lack the skills to relate to people in any other way. Being divorced from love puts these souls at a great disadvantage in relationships and, consequently, at a disadvantage in supporting themselves and making their way in the world.

Before the soul can go on to developing more complex skills and relationship skills, it has to learn to take care of such basic needs as food, water, housing, warmth, and protection. The earliest lifetimes provide the youngest souls with experiences that teach the value of hard work perseverance, patience, endurance, responsibility, caution, realism, and practicality, all necessary to survival.

Unless survival depends on it, very young souls spend little energy developing the intellect, and although everyone regardless of soul age has a certain ability to think, younger souls have little capacity for objectivity or rational thinking, which isn't attained until much later in the soul's evolution.

Very young souls are mostly found in agrarian, nomadic, or tribal cultures with strong family or community ties, where they perform simple tasks related to survival. But these types of societies are by no means only populated by very young souls. Older souls might also incarnate in similar settings for their own reasons. At this time, there are not very many newborn or very young souls on earth.

As you can imagine, life can feel quite overwhelming to newborn and very young souls, with so much to learn, so few relationship skills and coping mechanisms, and so little wisdom to draw upon, since wisdom, like everything else, is only gained through life experience.

The Stages of the Soul's Evolution

Most of the population of earth today is not that far advanced beyond the stage of evolution just described. This world is mostly populated by young souls, although not as young as just described, but far younger than most of you reading this. The majority of the souls in your world today are young souls who are striving for power and other egoic accomplishments, while older souls are seeking knowledge, understanding, personal and spiritual growth, peace, love, unity, and equality for all.

There are several stages the soul goes through in its

evolution, each with quite different lessons, goals, values, and perceptions. People *don't* see eye to eye, largely because they're looking out of different eyes. They see the world differently according to their soul age. They believe different things and want different things, and these differences create misunderstandings and conflicts.

Those in one stage of evolution don't understand those in the other stages and often have judgments about them. I hope the following information will help you understand each other better and bring more tolerance to your relationships, for people aren't able to be very different than they are. Eventually, they'll evolve out of their more limited beliefs and perceptions, but that may take many lifetimes. In the meantime, it's important to accept others and allow them their lessons and do your best to teach and uplift others when that's appropriate and requested of you.

That said, here's a brief description of each of the stages beyond the newborn stage already described:

Young souls, like the youngest souls just described, look out at the world with fear and deal with the world through retreat or aggression. They seek to control others in various ways because they believe they know what others need, what others should believe, and how others should behave. Their capacity to love is tainted by possessiveness and a need to control others.

Young souls cling to the rigid beliefs they've been taught, religious and otherwise, and believe everyone else should think like them. They're narrow-minded, not open to new ideas, and authoritarian and hierarchical. They're rigid, opposed to change, and cling to the past. Their intellectual interests are narrow, with little interest in anything that doesn't immediately affect themselves and their safety and comfort.

Needless to say, these traits are not compatible with what life requires to be happy, which is flexibility, open-mindedness, objectivity and a rational approach, a live-and-let-live attitude, and the humility to admit that you don't know very much. Unfortunately, the soul doesn't learn these things until well into its evolution—beyond the stage that most of humanity is at.

Souls that are a little older than this are less concerned with set beliefs and morals and more concerned with getting what they want, whatever that takes. They're self-centered and determined to have their way, and they adjust their beliefs and morals to serve their goals. They're less family oriented than souls younger than them and more interested in independence and self-development than accommodating others.

At this stage of evolution, the ego is at the height of its power, and the ego's goals are what matter most: beauty, power, attention, comfort, recognition, prestige, wealth, pleasure, and success. These individuals are competitive, action-oriented, and driven to succeed and to seek pleasure, which they do by drinking, watching movies and television, listening to music, dancing, sex, games, and sports.

Those at this stage have more of a live-and-let-live attitude than younger souls as long as others don't interfere with their goals and with getting what they want. They also have a stronger intellect and more skills, including better relationship skills, which they use to gain power and the material comforts they so desire, generally without much concern for others beyond their immediate circle of friends and family. Even with their intimates, love is transactional and all about getting their needs met. The lover is an object of gratification and a source of security. And yet, much is learned at this stage about love, if only through failing.

These are the shakers and movers, who are often found in positions of power, running corporations and governments or wielding power in other ways that benefit themselves. They feel little allegiance to the well-being of others or even to their nation. "Survival of the fittest" is their guiding principle and their excuse for caring mainly for themselves. They'll take whatever they can for themselves, usually within legal constraints, but not always. For many at this stage, their only interest in government is in how they can manipulate it or structure it to benefit themselves. Does all this sound familiar? This is the state of consciousness of the majority of people on earth at this time.

Souls that are older than this, more mature souls, begin to be interested in what makes themselves and others tick and what makes society and social structures work. They are the bureaucrats, social workers, educators, psychologists, professors, scientists, innovators, and other free-thinkers who are interested in contributing to society in meaningful ways. They are humanitarian, promoters of democracy and equality for all, and interested in serving their fellow human beings. They also might be artists, musicians, dancers, or others with significant talents, which have been developed over many lifetimes.

Unlike younger souls, those at this stage of evolution are thoughtful, more self-aware, and willing to take responsibility for their flaws and mistakes. Their engagement in self-analysis and introspection often leads to a certain angst and anxiety that younger souls rarely feel. The majority of your world's population is obviously not at this level yet, although many people are.

In the next and last stage of the soul's evolution, the focus is on understanding the meaning of life, gaining wisdom and compassion, growing in love and expressing that through service, developing extrasensory abilities, and transcending the ego. Old souls have little drive for success in the usual sense unless it furthers their life purpose. They are driven, instead, by a longing to experience their true nature and return Home.

In this stage, one learns to detach from the ego and voice in the head and eventually transcend negative emotions, which are supplanted by peace, love, joy, and acceptance. For old souls, love is more inclusive and impersonal, extending even to so-called enemies. Love as they know it is closer to unconditional love, although this is an ideal and rarely a constant in anyone's life. By the end of this stage of the evolutionary journey, the personality is recognized as a vehicle for soul development, and the true self and oneness with others is experienced more commonly.

What to Do About Differences

The implications of these differences in perspectives for your world are enormous. You often think that your problems stem from differences between races and cultures, but the differences in soul ages are responsible for more significant differences than race or culture. Many of your differences are masquerading as racial and cultural differences but are really differences in perceptions and values due to soul age. Your religious and political differences, for instance, are largely related to soul age.

Each race and nation is made up of a variety of soul ages. Races and nations are not homogeneous by any means but a mixture of soul ages, just as families are. You have much more in common with those at the same stage of evolution than you do with many in your same race or country or even your own family. Those at the same stage of evolution are the ones who understand you and who can most easily support you and cheer you on.

Those are the ones you enjoy being with. They are also often the ones who are important to fulfilling your life purpose.

Everyone around you—your neighbors, family members, friends, and the people you work with and who work for you and serve you in various ways—has a unique perspective on life and on the world that has been shaped by many things, not the least of which is their soul age. You can learn from them and they can learn from you. This is how it is in this enormous schoolhouse called earth. You are all thrown together to learn from each other. There is no mistake in where any soul is at; it is all as it's meant to be, and it can be no other way.

The differences between you and others must be accepted, and they are accepted more easily when you understand that souls are at different stages in their evolution and can't think or believe or feel other than the way they do. Yes, they will grow and evolve, but evolution is always very slow. You must be patient with each other, accept each other, and allow people to learn what they need to learn in their own way and at their own pace. Allow them to make their mistakes and learn from them, and also be available to help them learn if they ask for your help.

Regardless of what you believe, it will be difficult to find many people, if any, who believe exactly what you believe. Differing beliefs make each of you unique, and different beliefs and perspectives make life and people interesting.

People having different beliefs doesn't have to be a problem, unless the beliefs, themselves, infringe on other people's freedom to believe what they do and make the choices they do. As long as your beliefs don't infringe on other people's freedom and as long as they respect other people's uniqueness and humanity, beliefs don't have to be a problem.

The freedom to believe what you choose to believe is, perhaps, the most basic freedom. Without that, you won't be free, no matter how free other aspects of society might be. Without that freedom, you'll be ruled by beliefs imposed on you from others, either the state or a religion or a particular individual. This is dangerous and unhealthy for a society or nation.

An important task of human evolution is learning about the power of beliefs in one's life—for good and for ill. This is a basic and essential lesson for all human beings, and they need the freedom to explore this. People must have the freedom to choose what they believe and experience the consequences of those choices, as long as those beliefs don't interfere with other people's freedom to believe what they believe.

The problem is that most people are brought up with detrimental or limiting beliefs, without realizing that they can believe something else and fare much better. Those being brought up in rigid belief systems suffer because of their faulty beliefs, without realizing the cause of their suffering. They believe that they must believe those beliefs—or else. They're told that something terrible will happen to them if they question those beliefs, when in reality, the beliefs themselves are causing their lives to be more painful and difficult than their lives need to be. Their beliefs are causing them to suffer, but they're afraid that not believing them will cause them even greater suffering. They don't know what it's like to live according to truer beliefs, ones that don't cause them to suffer and that allow them the flexibility to learn from their own mistakes.

As you all know, some beliefs lead to bad results, both personally and societally, while other beliefs reap beneficial results. You are meant to discover which beliefs help you as an individual and a society and which ones hinder. You are meant to discover for yourselves the rules by which to live.

You are given some help in this by those who are wiser, who've come before you and written down what they discovered. They learned the truth about life, meaning they discovered the rules by which to live that ensure that you and society thrive. They know which beliefs work and which ones don't. Some of that wisdom is recorded in religion, but unfortunately religion is also full of beliefs that are not helpful, mistaken beliefs that cause great suffering.

We, on higher dimensions, are available to point you toward beliefs that will lead to greater happiness, peace, and love, and many of you are applying these beliefs and discovering the truth of them. This has been necessary because most of you've been given beliefs by parents and others that were not helpful, ones that didn't help you fulfill your greatest potential and be the best person you could be.

Surely, those people meant to give you the "right" beliefs, but how could they if what they, themselves, were taught was faulty? Most people don't question the beliefs they were given—they don't test them—largely out of fear of going against what they were taught. Consequently, many never find their way to the truth.

That doesn't have to be your fate. You can question your beliefs and replace ones that are limiting and negative with ones that help you flourish. Beliefs that help you flourish are, surely, also good for society. There are beliefs that are truer and work much better than others, and your task is to find your way to them by being open enough to question what you've been taught and replace any beliefs that take you away from love and peace with ones that take you to love and peace.

That is the measuring stick for truth that we have to offer: Keep the beliefs that take you to greater love and peace and throw out the ones that take you into fear, negativity, limitation, hatred, anger, or confusion.

That's a lot of beliefs that you can throw out! Indeed, you don't need that many beliefs to live the life you're meant to live, to be the best human being you can be. The beliefs you keep will also be ones that allow others to live the life they are meant to live, because beliefs that lead to love and peace will always include beliefs that allow others to relax and be more loving and peaceful.

So, what are you to do with those who believe very differently than you, especially when those beliefs steep them in hatred, division, anger, blame, resentment, and other negative emotions? The answer is that you can only do so much about other people's choices. You must respect their free will and allow them to make their choices and learn from them. That is our relationship with you as well. Everyone is learning and evolving, and everyone is making mistakes and suffering over their mistaken beliefs. Human evolution is messy, and you must accept this and allow it to be messy.

You can best cope with mistaken beliefs—ignorance—and the suffering those beliefs cause by "forgiving them for they know not what they do." This is not condoning their choices nor is it letting them wallow in their own negativity. By forgiving them, you are actually helping them—you're helping to free them from their own negativity by not adding any of your own negativity to theirs.

Sometimes the best you can do is not add any more negativity to the situation, since you're unlikely to change most people's minds by confronting them or even speaking rationally to them. When people are caught up in a negative egoic state, they can't be reasoned with, and they don't want your reasoning. They aren't open to facts or advice or teachings that might contradict their beliefs. If they ever come around and express an interest in you sharing your perspective, then share it, but until then, there isn't much point in trying to convert the unconvertible.

Those deeply entrenched in egoic beliefs and negative emotions will not welcome your love and light, although kindness toward them is certainly the best response. Still, they may resent your kindness, your love, and your peace. When people are in a negative state, they'll try to make you wrong no matter what you say.

So, "forgive them for they know not what they do." This allows you to unhook from their negativity and not take it on and to "let go and let God," meaning let go of any fear around this and rest in knowing that, given their circumstances and level of evolution, it would be impossible for them to be any other way in this moment, and that you can do little about this and that, in fact, "it is all good," all in God's hands.

Truly everything is unfolding as it needs to, and you can surrender any concerns or fears around this, since those only draw you into negativity. In these times, it's more important than ever to keep your vibration high, to remain as positive in your outlook as possible, and not let other people's negativity affect you. If that means disengaging from such people or from social media, then that may be the best course of action.

Let others be as they are. Changing their beliefs is not your responsibility unless they invite you to share your understanding with them. "Live and let live" is an example of a positive philosophy to live by, which means let people live their lives as they choose, including letting them believe what they believe, and trust that they'll learn and evolve as a result. This live-and-let-live philosophy is foundational to democracy, which celebrates such freedom, indeed, demands it.

What I mean by "it's in God's hands" is that this life that you've been given is being divinely guided toward greater love, and no matter how long it takes, life will take everyone to greater love, albeit by way of some suffering. Suffering eventually points everyone home to love.

So, if you meet someone who is hateful, angry, or afraid, they deserve your compassion because it's very painful to be in such a state. Giving them compassion and disengaging from trying to change them or bring them down in any way will free you from their negativity and help you maintain a positive state, which will be most conducive to transforming the ugliness that exists in your world. Going to battle with evil will only embroil you in conflict with those you wish to change, and that will not change them.

Raise yourself up by being the best person you can be and keep your vibration up by not engaging in whatever is causing others to be hateful, angry, and fearful. There's no need for that now. The best thing you can do is to question any beliefs that bring you into a negative egoic state and to affirm any beliefs that raise you out of that state. That is your work, not to change others but to change yourself. That is who you're responsible for.

You're responsible for your own consciousness, not other people's, and in the end, the only way that consciousness will be raised on earth is by raising others up to your consciousness through resonance, not so much by trying to reason with them. Consciousness is raised through loving kindness and acceptance. You can rest from any battle now. There can be no political, religious, or racial battle without two sides engaging in a battle. Do not engage in conflict, and those who wish to will have nothing to fight.

Compassion is a power you all have within you to tap. It is one of your superpowers. But, as with some superheroes, you may not be fully aware of this power. So, I'd like to make you more aware of it.

I'm not exaggerating when I say this is a superpower. What makes compassion a superpower is that it is powerful *and* highly available. It is inborn and requires no development. It is ever-present and ready to serve you whenever you need it. And it's easy to use. It requires no effort, only an awareness of it and a willingness to use it.

Usually, the only thing in the way of using your compassion is not realizing the value of it. If you don't use it or use it often enough, you might not be aware of its power in your life. It's in using it that you discover that compassion is powerful. But like a lot of things, it's easy to take compassion for granted and not fully use it. It's easy to forget that it's there and easy to forget to use it. So, I'm here to remind you of it.

It might be helpful to name some times when using your compassion is called for, so I will do that. One of the most important times to use this superpower—to practice compassion—is when you feel bad about yourself. Compassion needs to start with yourself, or you'll never be able to feel real compassion for others. How you treat yourself is how you'll treat others, and how you treat others reflects how you treat yourself. So, we must start there.

How do you treat yourself? What is the tone of the voice in your head like most of the time? Does it scold, push, criticize, judge, shame, compare? It probably does all of these things. Do you realize that this isn't a true voice, a voice that says anything true about you or even anything useful? Do you realize that you don't have to pay attention to it?

The trouble is that if you believe this voice, you become what it says you are to some extent. For example, if it tells you that you're better than others, then you'll see yourself this way and treat others as less than. You become that because you believe that. Maybe others don't see you that way, but they likely will if you keep talking and behaving accordingly.

You may think that seeing yourself as superior is treating yourself well, but it isn't. It's a coverup for feeling bad about yourself, a defense mechanism. You're not really fooling yourself. When you see this about yourself, the remedy is compassion. Have compassion for the predicament of being a human being who has a voice in the head that misleads and creates false identities. That voice tells you things that aren't true, things that make you feel bad about yourself or puff you up as a compensation, and it makes you do things you later regret.

This voice isn't who you are. At your core you are a loving being who wants peace, love, and unity with all. Can you feel the truth of that? Of course, you can, if you stop a moment to find that within yourself.

You don't have to go to battle with this voice. What it needs is compassion. You see the voice in your head for what it is, and you have compassion for it. Then, you're freed of all its negativity and false identities. What a super power compassion is!

Seeing this voice for what it is but fighting with it can't free you from it. That just keeps you engaged with it, and not liking it won't help either. Seeing it for what it is, isn't even enough. You must also give the voice in your head your compassion. Compassion aligns you with who you really are and frees you from this voice. From the vantage point of compassion, you are able to experience yourself as other than this voice.

What is compassionate? What is capable of compassion? It is your true self. When you choose to give yourself—your false self—compassion, the false self dissolves and stops being a problem. You are free of that lie. The false self is a lie that spins and perpetuates lies. It spins the great illusion that you are a separate and lacking self, while the truth is that you are the Divine masquerading as a human being.

Compassion frees you from the illusory world of the ego. Free to be what? Free to be the divine being that you truly are. The truth sets you free to experience yourself differently: as good, kind, loving, and a blessing to others.

Compassion allows you to love yourself, and this spills over to others, because when you love yourself, you automatically love others. Compassion for yourself allows you to feel compassion for others, which is what you need to relate to them more positively and what they need to heal and love themselves. What other ingredient could accomplish such feats: loving yourself, loving others, and healing others? As I said, compassion is a superpower.

Compassion is also the antidote for every negative emotion you ever experience. Negative feelings indicate that you've bought into one of the ego's (the voice in your head's) lies. That's okay. That happens. But when you find yourself feeling sad, angry, upset, regretful, ashamed, or some other negative emotion, give yourself some compassion. It's hard being human. You deserve compassion, just as every other human being does. You are doing your best, and every other human being is doing his or her best in this messy, unpredictable world.

In truth, it's not that the world is so difficult or even that life is so difficult but being human—having an ego—makes it so. Every human being has a similar ego. No human being has ever been born who didn't have the programming we call the ego, which challenges even the strongest and most advanced souls. No one lives life perfectly. No one is a saint. No one never gets caught in the ego at times.

Everyone is doing their best with the knowledge and understanding they have of the ego and the human condition. You are fortunate to see the truth about the voice in your head because then it becomes easier to apply the solution: compassion. If you don't understand the problem—that the problem lies in the voice in your head—then how could you know the solution to this problem? But once you know what the problem is, you can apply the solution: compassion.

However, before you understand this, to the ego, compassion sounds weak. It doesn't make sense. Compassion doesn't seem like a solution to anything. Unless you realize that compassion is your ticket to another state of consciousness, you'll overlook compassion and think it's unimportant. You won't recognize the power in it.

Compassion shifts your consciousness from the egoic state of consciousness to your divine nature, your best self. Your default is actually to be your worst self! That deserves compassion, wouldn't you say! You were given a default that causes you to feel negatively and react to life and to others with negativity. That is not your fault, so this deserves your compassion. And others deserve compassion for this same reason.

This is not to condone the negativity perpetrated by the egoic state of consciousness but simply to state a fact. It's not your fault that you're programmed with negative beliefs that lead to negative emotions that lead to harmful and ill-conceived actions. This is the human condition, and it deserves your compassion. Once you know this, then you can be free of this chain of events: negative beliefs leading to negative emotions leading to negative actions. Compassion frees you from this chain. That's powerful! Compassion frees you to be your best self, because the truth is that you are not your worst self but essentially a good person capable of great and kind acts.

So far, I've suggested that you give compassion in two instances: to your negative ideas about yourself and to your negative emotions. The third instance is to give compassion to others for the same things that you give yourself compassion for. Are they behaving badly? They deserve your compassion. Are they feeling angry, hateful, or sorrowful? They deserve your compassion. Are they attacking you, blaming you, hating you, judging you? They deserve your compassion.

It's challenging to feel compassion toward others when they're treating you badly; and yet, that's what is needed to defuse the situation and heal others. Conflicts and upsets can only happen when *two* people are engaged in conflict and egoic behavior. Compassion is the antidote to any conflict. Summoning compassion within yourself in such a situation is not capitulation or enabling or being a victim but taking constructive action to shift the consciousness of the person who's attacking you or to, at least, avoid bringing your own consciousness down.

Your compassion may come in the form of kind words, words that show that you understand how that person could feel that way. Or compassion may simply look like staying calm and disengaging so that your consciousness doesn't fall victim to the other person's ego. Sometimes the best that your compassion can accomplish is to remove you from the situation and allow the situation to de-escalate rather than risk getting your own ego involved. Later, your compassion might be expressed as forgiveness, either silently within yourself or reflected in your actions toward the other person after things have calmed down.

"Forgive them for they know not what they do." This is as true as it has ever been. So many are lost to their own egos without even knowing what that means or what to do about it. They're victims of their programming with no understanding of this or clarity about how to change that. The truth is out there, the answers they need, but they don't even know that.

You are the lucky ones because you have stumbled upon the Truth. How many lifetimes did it take? And so, it will take others many lifetimes before they're ready and willing to see the Truth. This time is shortened for some, as human evolution is being accelerated. And yet, for the most part, humanity remains at quite a primitive level, even after two thousand years and much technological development.

Those of you who know the Truth must count your blessings and share with others as you're able and have compassion for those who don't understand what you do.

How to Raise Your Vibration and Speed Up Your Evolution

Although you can only do so much about other people's evolution and state of consciousness, you can do something about yours. You can accelerate your evolution by cooperating with the natural unfolding that is already occurring in your life. Your soul is unfolding your life and seeing to your evolution, and all you have to do is come into greater alignment with that.

For that, you'll need to use your intuition, intention, free will, and prayer to overcome the momentum of old habits and egoic programming. You'll need to learn to detach from the voice in your head and listen to the still, small voice within instead. For this, your mind must be quiet, and this will also give you access to greater love and peace. What follows is some information about meditation and other practices that will help you do these things.

Meditation

Meditation is valuable because it strengthens one's ability to observe, detach from, and see the truth about thoughts and feelings, which frees you from the suffering they cause and heals the mistaken beliefs behind those feelings. Furthermore, when you gain some distance from the voice in your head, you begin to see that there's something much vaster and wiser than the ego available to run your life—the divine self—and it is content and in joy, awe, and wonderment of life. A regular practice of meditation will result in the happiness, peace, and contentment everyone longs for.

Meditation is the key practice that moves people out of the egoic state of consciousness into the experience of their divine self. It shifts your consciousness and aligns you with your divine nature so that you are expressing *that* in the world instead of your ego. You *become* your best self, your divine self, instead of your ego, and are more able to experience compassion, love, patience, and acceptance.

Meditation not only affects you while you're meditating, but how you are in your daily life. Over time, a practice of meditation will change your experience of yourself and of life and thereby change your life. It will bring you into a more positive inner state, one in which you are also in touch with your intuition and inner wisdom. This state is a very attractive one and attracts to you what you need, so life goes much more smoothly.

Meditation also promotes emotional healing. When you meditate, emotions may arise that were once repressed, such as anger or grief. When that happens, you don't need to do anything but allow the emotion to be there, experience it fully in the body, give it time to reveal itself, unwind, and naturally move on. These emotions just want to be fully experienced, and then they'll naturally dissipate. They are generally feelings you didn't allow yourself to fully digest, or experience, possibly because you were too young when they occurred and didn't know how to deal with them.

Fortunately, meditation is very easy to do, and I'll explain here what I think is most important for you to know about it so that you can make meditation a part of your life, if it isn't already. What's most important to understand about meditation is not so much how to do it, since it's really easy to do and there's nothing tricky about it, or even why, as long as you're convinced enough to do it, but how often. How often is everything when it comes to meditation. Meditation that you do only once in a while will only be so helpful, even if you do it for fairly long. What's important is that you meditate daily—at least once a day for forty-five minutes or more. The reason for this is that meditation is like training a muscle, and like muscles, meditation needs a regular workout or you get out of shape, in a sense.

What you're doing in meditation is training your brain to rest in another state, one other than the default state of consciousness, which is the egoic state of consciousness. To accomplish this, you have to spend time each day in a meditative state. Then, you stand a chance of making that state your default state, which is the goal of meditation.

A daily practice of meditation will make it possible to live in a much more relaxed and contented state: a state of

Presence—and this *is* possible. Plenty of people do live this way, but they probably meditate daily and have made living in Presence a goal.

It helps to know what your goals are—what your values are. What's most important to you? For most people, getting things done is a priority, and when that's the case, time spent in meditation is seen as a luxury, as unproductive, time they don't have. But that isn't true at all. Meditation is a necessity, not a luxury, as it makes everything a person does more effective, more efficient, and more enjoyable. It ensures that the time you do spend doing things is well-spent, as the choices you make from a state of Presence will be determined by your inner wisdom, not the voice in your head.

Once you become a regular meditator, some of the things that now take up your time might fall by the wayside. Many of the things that people do with their time are not as worthwhile as they seem, and meditation helps you see this, as you spend more time doing things that bring you joy and less time doing things that are about getting something your ego wants, such as shopping or working out or chatting with friends or watching television or YouTube. Most people spend a lot of time each day feeding the ego and little time feeding the soul. Once this changes, you feel different inside, and your life will change for the better. Living from Presence is a different state of consciousness and the goal of the spiritual path.

The point I want to make is that daily meditation is necessary to change your brain state more permanently. Without daily meditation, the changes the brain needs to make to become established in Presence are nearly impossible or would take a great deal of time. Spiritual evolution is slow, and there are two things that will speed it up: meditation and transmission. If you think that reading more books and absorbing more teachings will bring you the shift in consciousness you read about, then you're fooling yourself, for as important as teachings are, reading and listening to teachings will not change your brain, only meditation will.

So, briefly, I'll explain the basic technique of meditation. First of all, with meditation, it's important to be very comfortable so that you can meditate for an extended period of time without moving your body. This is more important than holding your body in an upright posture, as is so often recommended by yoga and meditation teachers. So, make yourself very comfortable so that you can rest in one position without moving. Reclining at a forty-five-degree angle, propped up with pillows in bed or in a reclining chair, will make it easier to meditate for an hour or more, which will enable your meditation to be much deeper.

Since meditation is essentially focusing your attention on one or all of the five senses, there are a few basic types of meditation. You'll need to experiment with each of them to see which one works best for you. They are:

Meditation on sound. Because you can't think and listen at the same time, listening is a natural and pleasant way of moving out of the mind and into the present moment. In a listening meditation, you focus on a particular sound, such as a bell, or on a piece of music, someone's voice in a guided meditation, a mantra, an affirmation, or a prayer that you repeat silently to yourself.

Repeating a mantra, which is traditionally a meaningful Sanskrit word or phrase, is a time-honored type of meditation. The mantra could be "Om" or "Om Shanti, Shanti, Om," or "Om Nama Shivaya." Another possibility is to choose your own word, phrase, or short prayer, something that is personally meaningful or resonates with you. Particularly powerful phrases are ones that evoke praise, gratitude, love, or simply relaxation.

Alternately, you can simply focus on the sounds in the environment as they arise. Listen to the sounds around you as if you are listening *for* something. Listening for something brings you into an attentive, alert, curious state of watchfulness.

Receive the sounds without mentally commenting on them. If you find yourself resisting a sound, such as a barking dog, notice that resistance and then bring yourself back to listening.

Alternately, listen to the silence in between the sounds and in between the thoughts. This silence isn't actually silent at all but has a certain sound. Also, notice how a sound emerges from this silence and returns to the silence.

You can also do a listening meditation to a beautiful, relaxing piece of instrumental music. Let yourself become fully immersed in the music.

Meditation on your breath. This is the most common type of meditation that's taught, but that doesn't mean it's superior to the other types of meditation or best for everyone. The best meditation is whatever works best for you personally.

Meditating on the breath is essentially a meditation, or focusing, on the sensations involved in breathing: Notice the feel of the breath as it enters your nose and leaves your nose. And, without changing how you breathe in any way, notice the movement of your chest and how the body breathes rhythmically in and out, effortlessly, softly, gently. If you find yourself thinking about your breathing, your body, or anything else, bring your attention back to the *experience* of breathing.

A variation on this is counting to a certain number on the in-breath, holding your breath for a certain count, and then exhaling to a certain count.

You can also try counting your breaths. Silently to yourself, count "one" on the in-breath, "two" on the out-breath, "three" on the in-breath, "four" on the out-breath, and so on up to ten. Then, repeat starting at "one." See if you can get to ten without losing your focus. If you lose your focus, start over at "one." This gives your mind one more thing to be busy with, which makes it less likely to wander.

One of the reasons meditating on the breath is such an effective way to meditate is that the breath and the mind are connected: When your breathing becomes slower and deeper, your mind becomes calmer and quieter. So, in addition to simply noticing your breath, you can also experiment with breathing more slowly and deeply and notice what effect that has on your mind.

Walking meditation. This is a meditation, or focusing, on the sensations involved in walking. Tai Chi, Chi Gong, and yoga, when yoga is done as a meditation, are other types of meditation similar to walking meditation that work well for those who are more kinesthetic and find sitting still challenging.

Meditation on beauty. Choose something beautiful in nature to look at and give it your full attention: a flower, a sunset, the breeze blowing through the trees, the clouds moving across the sky, or any other beautiful sight that has the capacity to capture your attention. Receive the visual impression and experience its impact on your being.

Alternately, move your gaze from object to object, without letting it rest on any one thing. This is an especially good practice for when you are walking in nature. Keep your eyes moving around your environment.

Meditation on energy. Those who are sensitive enough to feel the energy of the subtle body can meditate on these more subtle sensations by simply noticing them without doing anything about them, just noting them and letting them be.

Meditating on all the senses and subtle energy. This is a practice, usually done with your eyes closed, of simply noticing whatever you are noticing, whether it is a sound, a sensation, your breath, or subtle energy. You give your attention to whatever you're aware of and let your attention naturally move, as it will, from one sensory experience to another.

What's coming in through your senses right now? What are you experiencing? A sound? Warmth? Coolness? Air moving? Tension? Pain? Many sensations are likely to be happening at once. Notice them without evaluating them, commenting on them, or thinking about them.

When you do this meditation on sensing, what you realize is that your awareness naturally moves from noticing one thing to another. It moves from noticing a sound, to noticing a sensation, to noticing a thought, and so on. And, of course, sometimes awareness rests in one place for a while. *You* aren't doing this—your being is. In this meditation, you aren't controlling where your attention is going but simply noticing where it is naturally going—where your *being* is naturally directing it. The only thing *you* are doing is allowing awareness to go where it wants to go, and you're simply noticing that and enjoying that.

This type of meditation is also a good way to stay anchored in the present moment as you go about your day. During your day, make it a habit to pay attention to what you are sensing rather than to what you're thinking.

The basic instruction for all types of meditation is to focus as much as possible on whatever you've chosen to focus on: your breath, your bodily sensations, your mantra, sounds, energetic experiences, or what you're seeing. Inevitably, thoughts or feelings will arise, and when they do, notice them, and then put your focus back onto your mantra, your breath, the words in a guided meditation, the sounds in the environment, the sensations and energetic experiences in your body, or a combination of the above. Whenever you catch yourself caught up in a thought, gently bring yourself back to your point of focus. Eventually, you'll catch those thoughts when they first arise before you get caught up in them, in which case, you notice any thoughts as they arise and then return to focusing on whatever you are focusing on.

The instructions for how to meditate are no more complicated than that. What's hard about meditating is doing it regularly and for long enough in one sitting to shift your consciousness. It takes most people, especially beginning meditators, forty-five minutes or more before they drop into a deeper state. You'll know when you have dropped into this state because it feels a certain way, which is difficult to describe, beyond calling it a shift. Once this happens, stay in that state a while, the longer the better. At that point, you may be able to drop your meditation practice and just experience the state that the practice has taken you to.

To quit meditating before you drop into that deeper state will undermine your practice of meditation because meditating won't be as rewarding. Once you are able to drop into this state more quickly and easily, you'll find yourself looking forward to meditating, and then making time to meditate each day will be much easier. But first, you often have to make meditation a priority and make a commitment to doing it daily for forty-five minutes or more before it becomes a joy. Many people give up on meditating simply because they haven't stayed with it long enough and done it frequently enough to make it rewarding.

I would also like to add that there's no such thing as a bad or failed meditation. Every effort you make to meditate is worthwhile and matters, whether you're aware of any results or not. Try not to hold goals in regard to your meditation, such as having a particular spiritual experience or developing in particular ways you've heard about from others. Meditation will change you in ways that may not be readily apparent. Spiritual progress is a mysterious thing, and the mind isn't able to assess or evaluate one's progress. The mind loves to tell the story that you aren't making any progress, so why continue? So, watch out for the ways your mind might try to discourage you. Of course, the mind doesn't want you to meditate.

Those guiding you in other dimensions are aware of your efforts to meditate, and these efforts signal them that you are committed to your spiritual growth. When they see your commitment to meditate, they'll concentrate more of their energies on helping you with your spiritual progress.

Please do not underestimate the involvement of spiritual forces. Know that when you set aside time to meditate, you draw to you assistance from other dimensions. They are assisting you in healing and elevating your consciousness.

So, be sure to ask for their help before you start meditating. It's always helpful to say some sort of prayer that expresses your sincerity to heal and progress spiritually and one that calls forth help from other dimensions. Meditation is a time for becoming closer and more connected to those who are guiding you. Know that they are there supporting you in your efforts and ask them for help when you feel you need it.

A Practice to Help Silence the Mind

I'm sure you're all interested in having a quieter mind, and I have a practice for you that will help with that. Like all practices, this one is very easy. The hard part is remembering to do it. So, that will be up to you. The more you do this practice, the more automatic it will become, which is also true of all practices.

So, here it is: As you go about your day, or even in meditation, when a thought arises about the past, the future, another person, or anything else that presumes to know something, say to yourself: "I don't really know that" or "Who knows?"

The reason this practice is so powerful is because so much of what runs through the mind is speculation about things that can't be known. This practice helps you see this about the mind and break the habit of wanting to know things you can't know and thinking you *can* know such things. You'll be surprised at how many thoughts you have that assume to know something you couldn't possibly know.

The voice in your head chats with you throughout your day and often pretends to be wise and all-knowing. Opinions are an example of this. More often than not, the mind's opinions are not very well founded, and yet they're felt strongly and expressed with great certainty. The mind loves to form opinions and try to inform you about things, as if it knows. The mind is a con artist in this way: It pretends to be something other than it is, which is just programming.

I've often likened the egoic mind, the voice in your head, to the Magic 8-ball some of you played with as children, where you ask it a question, shake the 8-ball, and a "yes" or "no" or other phrase would show up as the answer. Even though the 8-ball's answers were random and had no wisdom behind them—even though this toy didn't work!—it was very popular because people would love to have something that could give them answers like this. It's in your egoic nature to want answers to everything.

Well, your very own mind is happy to supply you with an answer to any question or a response to any other musing that crosses your mind—no matter that the answers are made up, like the Magic 8-ball. The mind is very curious, after all. It has lots of questions and would like to know everything about everything and everything about others: what they're thinking, what they're feeling, what they might do, how they feel about you, how worthy they are to be your friend, what potential for relationship might be there. Enquiring minds want to know! Egos want to know.

And not unlike the "National Enquirer," the mind makes up answers to please itself! It assumes things and fabricates things to satisfy itself, enhance itself, feel safer, feel superior, make itself happy, or even make itself mad, since the ego actually enjoys being angry and stirred up emotionally in other ways.

Stirring up emotions is the purpose of some of the answers the voice in your head gives you to things you might wonder about. The ego loves drama, and so the ego loves to assume negative things about others or about a situation just to feel some emotion. The ego is in the business of stirring up emotions, and much of its commentary is designed to do that.

Then once you feel angry or sad or jealous or afraid, the ego can play the role of the wise, helpful friend who gives you advice for dealing with the negative feelings it just stirred up: "Get a cookie, and then call your friend and tell her what just happened." Or it might advise, "You should never talk to that person again!" And then, it offers several reasons for not talking to that person again: "He's not like you at all. He doesn't understand you. He's probably from the East coast. He probably had an abusive childhood," and on and on. All speculation. All made up!

You can stop this train of thought that the ego so happily engages in before it gathers speed and catches you up emotionally by countering it with the truth: "I don't really know that." It's actually very easy to see that a thought isn't true. You can't fool yourself that easily if you don't want to be fooled. It's just that people aren't generally aware of their thoughts and don't question their validity.

People assume their thoughts are true. How interesting! If this weren't so, you'd see through the ego quickly. It would be obvious that something very weird is going on inside your head! It's surprising that people don't question this voice and see how detrimental and often silly and irrational it is. The only explanation is that you're programmed to believe the voice in your head, and that's the truth. You're programmed to believe the programming that is the ego and the voice in your head.

So, if you don't really know if something's true, will you believe it anyway? The ego will. Many people continue to believe things they aren't sure about or things they simply want to believe. To the ego, it doesn't matter if something is true or not. To the ego, pretending to know is as good as knowing, since it doesn't want to admit to not knowing something. That would look stupid or weak, and the ego will pretend to be smart and strong even when it doesn't know something. Knowing, or at least pretending to know, is a survival strategy, and the ego is all about survival and coming out on top.

But *you* — the one I'm speaking to right now — knows better than to believe just anything without adequate evidence. You are not the irrational ego. You have an ego, but you are not your ego. And the proof of this is that you can see the truth in what I just said. What sees the truth and is willing to see the truth?

You can choose to believe something that you don't know to be true and can't know to be true, and plenty of people do this. That's your choice, although most people aren't consciously choosing to be fooled by their own mind. But if you're in your right mind, meaning if you're aligned with your divine self and not the ego, believing something that isn't true won't be acceptable or interesting. Unlike the ego, your divine self can't be anything but honest and beholden to the truth.

The egoic mind wants to know things that it can't know, but the divine self is content with life and with not knowing things. It accepts that certain things can't be known and doesn't try to know such things. Your divine self knows that it doesn't need to know what it doesn't know and that if it needs to know something, that knowing will arise.

Does this feel airy-fairy to you? That would be the ego's take. The ego doesn't trust that it will be all right if it doesn't know something. Not knowing is scary to the ego, and it doesn't like being scared, so its solution is to make something up. Now, that's truly airy-fairy.

It's pretty interesting to see what the mind makes up in the face of not knowing. This practice of saying "I don't really know that" or "Who knows?" or something similar will help you see how the ego lies to itself over small things as much as big things.

The egoic mind, after all, is the maker of an imaginary reality, and it cares nothing about reality. In fact, it runs from reality. Why? Because when you firmly land in reality, those types of thoughts are seen to have no purpose, no reality. The thoughts of the voice in your head are only of interest and relevance to the ego, because their purpose is to entrap you in the ego's imagined reality, which is not reality.

What is reality without thoughts? Just this. Just this simple experience of breathing, of seeing, of hearing, of touching, of smelling, of tasting, and of sensing on deeper levels. And what is there to sense on deeper levels? Love, peace, joy, compassion, courage, strength, hope, faith, curiosity, inspiration, intuition, wisdom, beauty, immense spaciousness, connectedness, contentment, aliveness, vibration, energy.

When you are fully in reality, in Presence, you feel soft, open, relaxed, spacious, and at one with life, as life moves you easily and naturally from one thing to the next. If life is moving you with such intelligence and ease, then what is there to know? Knowing naturally happens as part of reality, but the *experience* of reality is what counts, not any thoughts about it. With the mind, it's the other way around. Reality is co-opted by the mind with its thoughts about reality and everything else.

Yes, thoughts are part of reality and come and go like everything else that arises out of the Now, but they don't satisfy you or bring you joy like breathing, seeing, hearing, and sensing in other ways does. These are *experiences,* real experiences, while thoughts interrupt experience and take you out of experiencing and land you in an imaginary reality, one cut off from reality.

Your creative imagination and rational thought processes are valuable tools, but the voice in your head is something else. It is actually anti-life, anti-reality, and anti-love. It is your nemesis, and it's best to see this now. The voice in your head is not your friend, and it's particularly not a wise and helpful friend.

So please, dear ones, do this practice: In response to the voice in your head telling you something with authority or expressing an opinion, stop and assert: "No, I don't really know that. I really don't know." Then, just notice in your body how that feels to acknowledge that you don't know. Finally, you can just relax and let everything be as it is. You don't know and you don't have to know. What a relief!

A Prayer and Practice

I'd like to talk with you about Light, the Love and Light of the Creator, which is available to all who ask. Of course, you all know what light is. Light makes it possible for you to see everything in the world and for everything that's alive to thrive and grow. Light *is* life. Light is the physical manifestation of the Love and Light of the Creator.

The Love and Light of the Creator gives life to Life. Much of what you often take for granted is actually the Love and Light of the Creator at work in your world. For example, when you feel joyful or when you feel love, that is the effect of the Love and Light of the Creator moving through you. Or when you meet someone who's very special to you, the Love and Light of the Creator brought you together. Or when you create something wonderful, the Love and Light of the Creator made that possible. Or when you create a child or foster life in other ways, the Love and Light of the Creator made that possible.

This Love and Light is the life force that sustains and moves all life. It permeates all that is. It is the substance behind all that is. You could say that you *are* the Love and Light of the

Creator and so is everything else. You are immersed in a sea of Love and Light, and you don't even know it!

Just as the ocean sustains the creatures within its depths, you are sustained by the Love and Light of the Creator. This is not a metaphor. You are literally swimming in an ocean of Love and Light. And you *are* the ocean as well. There is no separation between the ocean and you. There is a permeable membrane between you and this ocean of Light, between all living things and the ocean of Love and Light that they "swim" in.

So, let's take a moment now and see how you experience this Love and Light within your being. To experience it, you have to be very still and focus on the subtle sensations in your energy body. You have a body that is flesh and bones, and you have an energy body that surrounds and interpenetrates your physical body. That is what I want you to tune in to right now. Just make this intention now to tune in to the subtle energy body that sustains you and connects you with all that is, and then focus your attention on any subtle sensations you may be aware of. Let's do this for a moment…

Most of you were probably aware of a vibration, however subtle. That's energy. Energy vibrates. This energy is the Love and Light of the Creator. You could say that this sea of energy is the Creator's body or the Creator's breath, which breathes life into all forms and is all forms. This energy is alive. It's a current of life that surrounds you and is ever-renewing itself. It is not static but ever-changing and ever-renewing and flows to you and from you, connecting you with others and with all life. Life is fed, renewed, and healed by this current of energy that is ever-present, ever-available, and always supporting you.

One of the features of this energy is that it can be and is affected by your intention, your will—not the will of the ego but your divine will. There's a big difference. Your personal will, the ego's will, contracts your energy and causes it to coagulate and stagnate, as the ego's will often opposes the natural ebb and flow of this current of life. But you have another will: the will of your divine self, which wishes only health and happiness for you. It brings you what you truly desire, what your divine self or soul's plan intends for you, and it removes what's no longer of service to your soul's growth.

That's why divine will sometimes looks like loss. Sometimes, this current of life removes things from you that your ego doesn't want removed or things which your misunderstandings try to hold in place. When this happens, this may feel like a loss when it's actually a gain. Some things, including people, may have to be removed from your life so that they can be replaced by something else you need. There is only so much room in your life, and sometimes space has to be made for something new to arrive into your life, something you never imagined or intended for yourself but which will play an important role in the unfolding of your plan.

Many of the things that have happened to you are things you never thought would happen. So, obviously, you're not creating everything in your life, as important as your personal beliefs are. You are creators, but there's a larger act of creation happening on the part of the Creator that supersedes your imagination or what you may think you want or what you may think you like.

I have a prayer for you that will be helpful in aligning with whatever is in your highest good to receive, which takes into account this higher will. Here it is:

"I'm willing to have the experience that is designed for me today. I'm willing to learn and grow from everything that comes my way. I'm open to receiving the healing, help, and abundance that you want for me. I'm worthy and willing to receive from life and willing to expel or turn away from all that interferes with receiving life's bounty, healing, and assistance."

Then, after saying this prayer or something similar, take a few minutes to relax and allow yourself to experience, on a subtle energy level, the flow of Love and Light coming to you from the Creator. This prayer will activate this flow or increase its prominence. After stating such a prayer, it's possible to feel this flow because it's divine will for you to receive the healing, help, and abundance that is yours to receive. You just have to ask for it. Invoking it in this way will set in motion a current of Love and Light that will bring your greatest good to you. This is a natural law: "Ask and you will receive." That is what's meant by this statement.

Such an intention is always answered because you've opened to what is your divine birthright to receive. And, often, the only thing in the way is an unconscious block to receiving this to its fullest. Everyone receives healing, help, and abundance in the form of Love and Light from the Creator, which then sets gears in motion to bring this about in your life. However, not everyone takes full advantage of the availability of this Love and Light, usually because they feel unworthy or are just not open to the idea that any such thing exists, so in not asking, they keep the door somewhat closed to receiving what is their due. In believing that help, healing, and abundance are available to you for the asking, you fling the door open to receiving this to the fullest amount that is possible given your lessons and your soul's plan.

Although it's true that there are times when you're meant to experience a health crisis or other limitation and, therefore, what you receive when you state this prayer and make this intention may not appear to be the fullness you're asking for, you will receive in the ways you need to, to overcome any stumbling blocks you may be creating in your healing or in learning your lessons. So, in that way, you are receiving what you need, if not immediate healing or abundance.

You always receive what you need, especially if you ask to receive what you need without putting any restrictions on what that might look like. If you don't ask, however, then you are more on your own in life, and it's assumed that this is what you want, that this is your free will choice. If you don't want to be on your own to this degree, you have to specifically ask for the healing, help, and abundance you need in your life, and that will take whatever form is most appropriate at that time.

Do you see how asking is important? We, those on other dimensions, are always co-creating with you and helping you in ways we can, but it must be a co-creation. You must also align your will with what the Divine is co-creating with you so that it is a true partnership. So often, people are attempting to create one thing, while divine will is creating something else. Divine will and individual will may be at cross-purposes. But when they're aligned, then life will go much more smoothly, peacefully, and joyfully.

So, as a practice, may I suggest that you make this prayer or something similar a part of your day, that you make a clear statement each day of your intention to be aligned with divine will. You can create a shortened version of this prayer by saying something like: *"Thy will be done in this moment and always."* Or *"I am open, ready, and willing to receive whatever I need in alignment with my highest good and the good of all."* Or you can state any of the single sentences in the longer prayer that I've given you rather than the whole prayer. The specific words are not as important as the intention held in your heart. Once again, here is that longer prayer:

"I'm willing to have the experience that is designed for me today. I'm willing to learn and grow from everything that comes my way. I'm open to receiving the healing, help, and abundance that You want for me. I'm worthy and willing to receive from life and willing to expel or turn away from all that interferes with receiving life's bounty, healing, and assistance."

Practicing Kindness

Being kind requires something. It doesn't come automatically because being kind isn't natural to your default network, the egoic conditioning. The ego has a fight or flight mentality (fear or attack), and kindness is no such strategy for survival. And yet, kindness is the best strategy because it makes for cooperation between people.

Without cooperation, human beings would not and could not survive. You wouldn't be able to operate as a society. This is one reason the Golden Rule is so important and so respected: "Do unto others as you would have them do unto you." Without this level of morality, people cannot join together or stay together. So, it's easy enough to deduce what's lacking in your world today, since you're having such difficulty coming together as one world, indeed, even as one nation in many cases. What's lacking is old-fashioned kindness.

Kindness is the glue that holds societies, nations, families, and every kind of relationship together. Kindness requires a willingness to not react from your default, from the ego. Kindness isn't natural to human beings. It takes effort to choose to act kindly. Kindness requires stopping a moment and making a choice to be respectful toward another.

Respect is a component of kindness, a necessary ingredient. Without respect, being kind to others might simply be manipulation on the part of the ego to get what it wants. Kindness must come from a place of "I see you as an equal, and I know you to be good, and I'm open to discovering what good can come from knowing you."

Kindness is an extended hand to someone out of good will and an expectation of good will in return. In that sense, it's like an agreement. People within a society agree to be kind and cooperative with each other because this benefits everyone. This must be a given assumption within society—that you are working together toward the greater good. Without this tacit agreement, a society can't flourish and people within it can't thrive.

Kindness is more important than you may think, which is why I'm speaking about it now. It's easy to underestimate the power of kindness and, therefore, not make that extra effort to be kind. If you underestimate the importance of kindness, you're not likely to be kind. Kindness must be held as a high value, because it is the highest value. Kindness is the expression of a loving heart, and a loving heart is the key to happiness and the key to surviving well, both individually and as a society and a world. That's how important kindness is, for what value would love be if it weren't expressed?

Love is the greatest ideal and the greatest value, but it's nothing if it isn't lived, isn't expressed. Love that isn't lived is simply an idea about love. People talk about love and think about love, and churches preach love, but until love is lived, peace won't come to earth.

Every day, in every moment, you choose what's most important to you, and this is expressed in the choices you make about how you spend your time. But more important even than this is *how* you go about your day. Do you hurry through your day in the most efficient way possible, missing the opportunities to love? Or are you mindful about *how* you do the things you do? Do you do them with love and do you treat people with love?

What does it mean to do what you do with love? This means giving your full attention to what you're doing, as if what you're doing is precious or sacred, and doing what you do in a spirit of gratitude and joy. When you love something, you give your attention fully to it, and you give this attention out of gratitude and joy. This is love. Simply this.

I have often said, "What you give your attention to is what you love." When you give your attention to the voice in your head, you are loving those thoughts. You are feeding them, for whatever you give your attention to looms larger in your experience and becomes your experience. When you give your attention to your thoughts, you feed them, and those thoughts will stay as long as you give your attention to them and be fed by others, and those same thoughts will return another time.

On the other hand, if you give your attention to what's arising in the present moment, whether it's something you're doing or something you're hearing or experiencing in some other way, then you'll fully drink of that moment. The thing about being present in the moment is that the moment is constantly changing. Even if you're doing the same thing for a while, the experience is never the same moment to moment.

What you get when you give your attention to whatever you're experiencing is life—you get to experience your life, real life. However, the mind isn't interested in real life, so it naturally tries to draw you out of it and into its virtual reality. But life needs your attention! And when you give life your attention, you're rewarded with a richness, contentment, and joy that isn't possible in the egoic state of consciousness.

Of course, you won't know the joy and contentment of the present moment if you don't spend enough time in real life, which is the case for most people. They don't realize or appreciate the subtle joy and contentment that comes from giving their attention fully to the moment.

This is why meditation is so important. Without a practice of meditation, you barely touch into real life; you barely taste it. Before you'll want to stay in the present moment, you have to have a bigger taste of real life. Meditation gives you that taste, but more importantly, meditation makes it possible for you to be present in a way that isn't possible if you don't meditate.

Some people think, "I'll just be present. I don't need to meditate." But that's not how it works. Unless you meditate regularly, you won't be able to be present for long while you're going about your day because movement activates the mind. You also won't be motivated to be present. With a practice of meditation, being present throughout your day is much easier because meditation trains your brain to be in that state of consciousness. So, you practice being present in meditation to fortify that brain state so that when you're moving, when it's more difficult to be present, you'll still be able to be present.

This goes for practicing kindness as well. Kindness is a byproduct of being present. If you don't meditate, it will be more difficult to practice kindness in your life because the ego will still have a hold on you, and the ego isn't focused on kindness but on getting things done. The ego will push you through the day, and that isn't a state of presence and, consequently, not conducive to kindness.

Spiritual teachings point you to spiritual practices, such as meditation, because spiritual practices and meditation are necessary to be able to put spiritual teachings into practice. As I said, you can believe that love is important and you can read about it and talk about it, but that will only go so far in making you more loving. Something else is required, something beyond even wanting to be more loving. Plenty of people want to be more loving but don't succeed. Why not? Because they're living in a state of consciousness that is anti-love. How can love come from that? You have to begin to live in a state of consciousness where love is naturally expressed, and that state of consciousness is developed and arrived at through meditation and other spiritual practices.

There's one other point I want to make that is so important. The people in powerful positions in your world need to be people who are kind or who, at the very least, have this as a goal or value. This was true of most Christians in the past, but something has happened to Christianity of late, which undermines my most basic teaching. Just as the ego sees love as weak, some sects of Christianity now see love and kindness as weak. They are preaching the opposite of what I taught and calling it Christianity.

Any teaching that does not hold love, peace, and unity as the highest value is not what I taught, and that should be plain enough. A society cannot withstand divisiveness in its leaders — its teachers, preachers, politicians, and other influential voices. You must elect and follow only those who are kind and who lead with kindness and evict those who are separative, hateful, unkind, power-hungry, and see themselves as superior to others.

Chapter 4

Karmic Justice and Healing Traumas

This very lengthy chapter is being included in this book because it contains important and relevant information that I want to share with you about how the soul heals from trauma over the course of many lifetimes and the kind of karma those who harm others might meet as a result of their actions. If you find that the subject matter isn't of interest, you can skip ahead, since this chapter isn't integral to understanding the remainder of the book.

This information was part of another book this author channeled in 1997, called *Sojourn,* which is no longer in print. It was given to her by another being that I and other Ascended Masters work closely with. I hope you find it enlightening and healing.

Near Deaths and Traumatic Deaths

Brushes with Death

Close brushes with death are nearly always traumatizing. The importance of what happens following a scrape with death will be evident in the following stories. How an incident and its effects are handled determines how traumatized someone will be. But this isn't all that affects how a traumatic experience is internalized. The victim's astrology chart, previous experiences (including past-life experiences), gender, and age are also significant in shaping the victim's reactions to an event. All of these influence what psychological adaptations the victim makes.

Case A

This is the story of a girl named Alana who was brutally raped and left bleeding to die many lifetimes ago. Alana fought her attacker until she no longer had the strength and then fell unconscious. Her attacker left her for dead and escaped.

Very early the next morning, Alana was discovered by a traveler on the road where her attacker had left her. The traveler loaded her into his wagon, took her to a nearby house, and summoned a physician. After bandaging her, Alana was taken to her home, where she lived alone with her frail and somewhat elderly mother.

Her mother didn't ask any questions. She had seen this kind of thing before and thought it was improper to speak about it. She attended to her daughter meticulously, as she would anything that required her attention, but they never spoke about what happened.

Alana was thirteen years old and had never been with a man before. She felt terrified, confused, and alone. She saw no future for herself because she couldn't imagine ever being with a man after that. Unfortunately, Alana never knew her father, who had left her mother shortly after her birth, and there were no other men in her life to reshape her ideas about men. She lived only a few more years, succumbing to an illness common then.

Her next incarnation took into account her need for healing. Her astrology chart emphasized the element of fire to give her the independence, fortitude, and assertiveness to heal this issue. Her family named her Greta. This family was loving and large, one where nothing was too private or sacred to be discussed and where the parents were openly affectionate. And, Greta was attractive. The plan was obvious: to create circumstances in which romantic love could flower.

Although Greta's environment lived up to her soul's intentions, she still suffered as a result of her previous lifetime's experience. Despite Greta's fiery astrology chart, she was shy and withdrawn and had trouble sharing her thoughts. She was different from the rest of her family, but they accepted her and encouraged her to be more confident. Nevertheless, to fulfill her potentials, she would have to overcome her pain. There were no psychotherapists, shamans, witches, or other healers in her country, only priests. This left the healing up to those in her environment—and her soul.

One day, while sitting alone in a secluded spot on a hill, Greta had the sensation of being totally free and unfettered. She sensed she could do anything, that she could do something important. This was the first time she'd thought about anything other than her day-to-day existence and the possibility of marriage and a family.

As this sense within her grew, Greta was led to a family who had a daughter around her own age who was paralyzed. Greta visited the girl daily and read to her. One day, she was reading her a story about a dancer, and the girl began to cry. The paralyzed girl would never know what it was like to dance. This touched Greta and strengthened her appreciation for her own freedom and vitality. Circumstances were working to draw out

Greta's fiery energy.

Greta married. Her husband was a warm and loving man, robust and affectionate, much like her own father. But she had difficulty adjusting to the sexual aspect of their marriage. For some reason that she didn't understand, intimacy felt frightening and shameful. Nevertheless, with her husband's gentle encouragement and sensitivity, she learned to be more relaxed and trusting. She began to blossom as she saw her children grow into happy, free-spirited individuals.

Despite Greta's busy life, deep feelings of compassion moved her to visit the hospital regularly, where she chatted with the patients and shared her cheery disposition. Her shyness mellowed into a warm receptivity to the pain of others, and her friendliness and optimism gave others hope and eased their suffering. She realized she had a gift for helping others, which she used throughout the remainder of that lifetime.

In her next lifetime, she was a woman again. One more step was necessary to heal the wound inflicted lifetimes ago. The rape hadn't been part of her soul's plan then but interfered with it, which is why her soul left her body early through illness. The plan for this lifetime would be to recreate the situation, but with a favorable outcome. Her soul would try to arrange a situation in which her protests would release her from her attacker. Fighting back hadn't helped her before and resulted in feelings of helplessness. To increase the likelihood of success, her environment, astrology chart, and early experiences were carefully chosen.

This time, when the attack happened, she succeeded in freeing herself, which balanced her previous sense of helplessness. After this, she began helping other rape victims. This lifetime, instead of being one of victimization, became one of service and strength. She had come through this ordeal with greater compassion, fortitude, and faith in the human spirit.

Although you may not be able to understand the meaning of an event as it's happening, every event eventually leads to good, to a gift. What's hard to accept is that the gift of that event may not be apparent until other lifetimes. From an earthly standpoint, this is undeniably unfair. But from the soul's standpoint, life is not only fair, but something you've willingly and eagerly entered into.

Case B

A boy named Daniel was fishing with a friend on a riverbank. When Daniel tried to get to another fishing spot on the other side of the river, the current dragged him under. After being swept downstream a short distance, he resurfaced, where he grabbed a log and rode it to safety. In the meantime, his friend, who'd gone for help, returned with two men and a rope. They found Daniel resting nearby on the riverbank.

With hoots of gladness, they called and waved to him. He felt particularly alive—he'd escaped death! In school, everyone was interested in hearing about his misadventure, which made him feel like a hero. This event made a deep impression on him. He saw himself as a survivor, someone who comes out on top.

His next lifetime was as a female named Mary. Even as a child, Mary was bold and confident. Although her astrology chart didn't reflect this particularly, she exuded a rare confidence and self-satisfaction.

Mary lived in a small village where women and girls were expected to do domestic tasks while the men hunted, farmed, and provided in other ways. She was restless and discontent. She longed to be special. One day, while helping her father with chores in the barn, one of the animals kicked over a lantern and started a fire, which spread quickly. Mary grabbed a bucket of milk nearby and flung it, which dampened the blaze just enough to control it. At last, she had the admiration she longed for. Her subconscious belief in her ability to come out on top was reinforced.

In her next lifetime, the plan was to continue to develop her bravery and sense of mastery. So, her soul chose a male incarnation, circumstances that would demand courage and enterprise, and an astrology chart conducive to developing these qualities. Billy was the given name in this incarnation. Billy was born into a family that captured and broke wild mustangs. He loved going with his father to track, rope, and bring in the mustangs.

One day, while riding alone, Billy spotted a mountain lion sunning on a rock. He stopped, dismounted, tied his horse, and quietly climbed toward the lion, trying to get a closer look at it without it seeing him. The mountain lion caught his scent and charged. Billy didn't escape without a terrible swipe from its paws, gouging him across his arm. The mountain lion retreated, leaving Billy alone with his bleeding arm. Using his shirt as a bandage, he managed to get home.

When Billy arrived home, he was scolded, but also joyfully embraced. For some, this experience might have resulted in self-doubt or unconscious fears, but topping other successful brushes with death in former lifetimes, it contributed to his sense of mastery and invincibility. At this point, his soul may continue to create experiences to develop further courage and fearlessness or just find ways to use the courage he already has.

Traumatic Deaths

Traumatic deaths can be more psychologically damaging for the loved ones who survive than for the one who has died, especially if the loved ones witnessed the death. Nevertheless, traumatic deaths often leave the one who died with emotional scars that will need to be addressed in future lifetimes.

The extent of the damage and what will be needed to heal it depend on the circumstances and the individual's development. Of greatest importance is the state of mind at death. It helps if the individual found some inner peace and acceptance before death. If he or she died with strong feelings of fear, regret, anger, or sorrow, the assumptions underlying these feelings will need healing.

Healing a traumatic death nearly always entails working with the underlying beliefs about oneself or about life reflected in the prominent feeling at death. These beliefs and feelings are influenced by the astrology chart and all previous experiences. The importance of the state of mind at death will be obvious in the stories that follow.

Some healing also occurs between lifetimes on the astral plane. When you arrive on the astral plane after death, you are offered instruction, guidance, and healing, which prepare you for further healing on the physical plane. How effective this is depends on one's willingness to be helped.

When considerable damage has occurred or if someone is refusing help, he or she may sit out the dance of life for what would amount to several lifetimes before feeling ready to face another ordinary life of challenges or one designed for healing.

As an alternative to sitting it out on the astral plane, someone might choose a lifetime of ease. This is possible because the soul can block out wounds if that is advantageous. It does this by giving a directive to the unconscious mind to block recognition of the psychological effects of a particular incident. Although this is only a temporary measure to provide some relief from psychological pain, it can help build some psychological strength and distance from the offense, making healing in later lifetimes easier.

The following stories show how a traumatic death or the trauma from witnessing one might be healed.

Case C

A young boy named Ton-Ton was walking in the woods one day, when he came upon a trap meant for a large animal. Inside the trap, lay a man who was broken, bleeding, and gasping for his last breaths.

Ton-Ton was too small to help the man, so he did the only thing he could think of: He cried for help. Being very young and quite traumatized by what he saw, he didn't think of running to get help but stayed there crying. He continued to intermittently call for help and cry tearfully. Finally, around the same time a party of hunters found the distraught child, the man gave up his life.

If Ton-Ton had been older, he probably would have had the emotional resources to cope with the trauma and the intellectual wherewithal to have taken more effective action. As it was, he felt responsible for the death, and a sense of shame and guilt haunted him the rest of that lifetime.

To help him work through this, in his next lifetime, his soul would try to arrange for him to save someone's life, although trying to heal something this way is risky. An opportunity may never come or a lack of confidence may interfere with success. Selecting the right environment and astrology chart was crucial. Having done this, it was up to his soul to try to arrange the right circumstances.

The opportunity arose when he was in the military. In a

battle one day, he had the opportunity to save several men. He did manage to save one person but was deeply regretful over not saving the others. Fortunately, he was able to discuss his feelings with others who'd had similar experiences and receive support for letting go of the idea that he was responsible for the deaths of the others. He even received a medal for his heroism.

Although all of this helped, subtle feelings of guilt lingered on. To cope with these, he established a support group for surviving soldiers. So, his own need for healing gave birth to a means for healing many. He'd found a way to continue his own healing and transform his pain into service. He grew in compassion not only for others, but more importantly for himself. And with this compassion came forgiveness, the last step in the healing process.

Case D

This is the story of a man named Alexander who was tortured to death. As much as we'd like it to be otherwise, torture has been a constant throughout history. As long as humankind is ruled by the ego, such acts will persist.

What effect does an incident like torture have on someone's psyche? There's no one answer to this. Everyone internalizes experiences differently and in more ways than one. Alexander's death reinforced his conviction that his integrity was more precious than his life and that he was more than just his body. However, Alexander also internalized a sense of pessimism and futility, which he brought into his next lifetime. It's difficult to come away from a tortured death without some loss of faith in the goodness of humankind. In the scope of each lifetime, the good don't always win, and one can't help but be affected by this.

Alexander's next lifetime would be one that allowed him to

express the compassion he'd gained from his tragic death and continue his spiritual goal of service. Although the torturous death didn't prevent him from serving others in his next lifetime, it did prevent him from enjoying life more fully, as he felt a sense of ongoing heaviness. Since service without joy is closer to servitude than true service, he needed something to reactivate his joy and appreciation of life's blessedness.

In his next lifetime, his soul chose an astrology chart that supported fun, creativity, courage, and self-expression (Leo). It also provided circumstances of relative luxury, which freed him from the stress of survival and gave him opportunities for self-expression and pleasure.

Although he wasn't attuned to this playful, courageous, and creative energy, these energies still worked their magic on him. He gained a sense of control and mastery over life, which counteracted his former feelings of futility and powerlessness. Out of gratitude for his good fortune, he founded a school for unfortunate children that instilled spiritual values and gave the children opportunities for creative expression. This lifetime balanced his sense of futility, expanded his repertoire of behaviors, and equipped him to serve in a wider variety of ways than before.

Case E

While walking alone one day, Karen came across a man who'd been run over by a train. The sight was the biggest shock of her life. She became physically ill but managed to get herself back home and notify the authorities. Even though she didn't know the man and felt no responsibility for his death, it affected her deeply. At twenty, Karen's life was just beginning. Until this reminder, her own death seemed remote.

Karen responded to this tragedy by searching for a belief system that would help her be more comfortable with the uncertainty of life. Eventually, she discovered beliefs that brought comfort to her and helped her bring comfort to others. This resolved any negative effects this experience might have had on her.

Every experience, whether chosen for you by your soul or not, has the potential to further your growth and enrich your life. The result of any experience depends on your responses to it—the choices you make. Whatever the choice, it will eventually lead to growth, but some choices lead more gracefully to this than others. There is no blame in any of your choices. You are here to learn. Whether you make satisfying choices or painful ones, the outcome is eventually greater understanding.

Let's go back and look at this story from the victim's standpoint. He was also young, about the same age as Karen. He was walking from one town to the next along the railroad tracks when he decided he'd make better time if he hopped a train. He waited at a curve where the train would be traveling more slowly. Had he known better, he would have realized that this was extremely dangerous and likely to fail. When his opportunity came, he jumped, lost his grip, and fell under the train's wheels.

Because his death was so immediate, you might think it had little effect on his psyche, but at the moment of death, the mind takes in the entire experience and draws conclusions. In one split second, he recognized his folly and concluded that he had poor judgment. He carried this conclusion into his next lifetime.

In the lifetime that followed, he was careful and somewhat fearful. People said he was sensible and practical, characteristics that resulted from his former death and an astrology chart with plenty of Capricorn. His tragic death had taught him to be more cautious, and the careful choices he'd make in this lifetime would teach him that he could trust his judgment. By the end of this lifetime, his distrust in himself would be balanced and he would be wiser. In his next lifetime, he will undoubtedly act with common sense—and confidence.

Every soul makes similar mistakes. Experiences like these teach caution, common sense, and responsibility. Everyone must learn these things. Losing your life over something as seemingly preventable as poor judgment is never easy, but such incidents are part of life's lessons.

As we just saw, one's state of mind and the beliefs held at the moment of death are important. Your beliefs *about death* also affect your state of mind before death. Although some people don't fear death, they are in the minority. Most need some understanding about death and support at death to make this transition successfully. A lack of preparation for death can make leaving life more difficult as well as entering into a new life in other realms. Fortunately, people are beginning to realize the importance of preparing people for death when possible.

Death is always successful. No one has ever been unsuccessful in shedding his or her body. But dying successfully in another sense means coming to peace with one's life and one's death. There comes a time when you learn to die more consciously, when you know you are more than the ego, more than the experience of death, and more than the perspective held at death.

This realization comes to people at different points in their evolution, usually as old souls. When the time comes, the soul designs a method of death to bring about this realization. When death isn't actively engaged in teaching a lesson, such as better judgment, the soul might use death to make one more aware of one's spiritual nature. The lessons of life are many, and many of life's lessons are taught through death. Oddly enough, death is also a way of teaching people about their immortality, since that is what they discover on the other side.

Traumatic Accidents

The psychological impact of traumatic accidents is similar to that of traumatic deaths, except the need for healing has to be faced in that same lifetime. Unfortunately, sometimes the psychological effects of an accident become more entrenched instead of healed, and the remainder of the person's life is seen through the distorted lens of his or her victimization.

A person's attitude and willingness to recommit to life following an accident are integral to healing. The person has to be willing to see the future as worthwhile. This shift in attitude *is* the healing in many cases and may even be the reason for the accident. One's attitude affects not only one's capacity to heal, but the amount of psychological damage that results from an accident. Negative conclusions formed at the time of an accident can have a long-term psychological effect, just as those formed at the moment of death. If the person continues to hold those beliefs, they may become limiting and self-fulfilling. The stories that follow illustrate these points.

Case F

Lynn lost her young child and sustained serious injuries to her face and body in an automobile accident. Her only thought then was for her young daughter, who died instantly. Because Lynn hadn't been able to prevent her daughter's death, she felt responsible, even though there was nothing she could have done.

Lynn's fixation on her daughter's death caused her to be

despondent, which slowed her progress in physical therapy and dampened her motivation to have plastic surgery. Even though she had a loving husband, a son, and the potential for full recovery, she didn't care about living.

When these tragedies happen, people understandably wonder why. There is no single answer to this question. In this instance, both Lynn and her child had chosen this experience before their birth, although not every accident is prearranged like this. Even when an accident isn't part of the soul's plan, the soul can usually find a way to use it for growth and eventually turn it into a gift.

For Lynn, the accident was to be a way of counteracting her frivolousness and vanity. Because Lynn valued appearances too much, her soul designed this accident to help her realize the value of life beyond appearances. Such tragedies help people see that who they really are remains unchanged and what has changed is not really who they are.

The child, on the other hand, joined this family to further the family members' compassion and to advance her own understanding by dying this way. Early death is a lesson every soul chooses at some point. As difficult as it may be to see any benefit in a child dying, such a death does increase that soul's appreciation of life and motivation to live. As a result, early death is sometimes chosen by the soul to prevent a recurrence of suicide if someone has a history of that.

As might be expected, Lynn was angry and disheartened for some time. As her body slowly healed, she regretted losing her beauty and longed to be beautiful again. It took years before she accepted her fate and decided to get on with life in her new body.

She began by getting involved with an after-school project for disadvantaged youths, which gave her an outlet for expressing the love she had inside her for children. If she couldn't share her love with her lost child, she would share it with other children. In her next lifetime, she's likely to continue to serve in some way, using the compassion and understanding she developed from this experience.

Life is never easy. But at times, life is seen with clarity, and it shines with meaning. Just because this state isn't constant doesn't mean that life lacks meaning, only that this vision is hard to sustain. Sometimes it takes a tragedy to awaken one's search for meaning and open one up to the soul's wisdom. Once someone begins searching for the answer to, "Why me?" he or she is often led in unexpected and meaningful directions.

The wisdom and growth garnered from traumatic experiences can't be gained from books or even from others. Experience teaches life's lessons like no amount of study can. If you look back on your life, you can probably see that your greatest strengths have come from your greatest challenges. This is how wisdom is born, and no other way. Wisdom is a jewel born from pain.

Case G

Jan lost his arm in a farm accident. He was only ten and didn't have the emotional resources or family support to deal successfully with this loss. He concluded that his life would never be normal. If the accident had happened later in life, he might not have felt that his condition was so limiting.

This belief became a self-fulfilling prophecy, as do many negative beliefs. Jan's feelings of inferiority affected other areas of his life and became more handicapping than the disability itself. Others began seeing him as incapable too and compensated for him, reinforcing his sense of inferiority. After all, if others do things for you, not only do you not learn to do these things for yourself, but you may question your capability. Those who work with the handicapped know this and may have learned this from being handicapped themselves in a former lifetime. Many who are now handicapped may know this too from other lifetimes and have chosen to be disabled again to act as models for others.

At the end of this lifetime, Jan needed healing for the trauma he'd suffered and for a lifetime of unmet potential and feelings of inferiority. In his next lifetime, his soul chose a family that would help him develop his confidence and talents. This family had the material and emotional resources to give him a strong sense of self-worth and the ease he needed to recuperate from his previous lifetime.

With this as his foundation, he ventured into athletics. Physical prowess was something he'd developed in other lifetimes. His soul would use this and an appropriate astrology chart to rebuild his confidence. This lifetime built his physical prowess and psychological strength, which prepared him to face the lessons of disability again in his next lifetime.

For that lifetime, his soul chose another supportive family and, this time, an accident in which he lost his leg. The tragedy happened in his teenage years, just when he was beginning to excel in team sports. His love of sports carried him through this injury because he wanted so badly to participate in sports again. Every day he worked to build his strength so that he could support himself on one leg. Eventually, he developed a means of mobility that allowed him to run and compete in certain games. He would never be a professional athlete or excel as he might have before the loss of his leg, but he grew to be grateful for what he *could* do—and he never stopped dreaming of what he might achieve.

You may wonder why Jan found himself in a situation that

wasn't conducive to meeting the challenge of losing his arm. This is because losing his arm wasn't part of Jan's plan. Unintended accidents sometimes can't be prevented by the soul. As a result, the soul's initial plan had to be set aside. If his soul had decided that it was impossible to work within these circumstances, it would have left the body, but his soul saw a potential for advancement through these new circumstances. Just because Jan didn't advance doesn't mean he couldn't have or that his soul wasn't trying to help him. Unfortunately, the soul's tactics don't always work.

Case H

Jack became paralyzed after a fall. Although the paralysis wasn't part of his pre-life plan, it became part of his plan later. His soul created this accident to shift Jack's focus away from physical development, which was interfering with accomplishing his life purpose. Before life, Jack's soul and three others had agreed to collaborate on an invention, but Jack's exceptional athletic abilities were sidetracking him. To bring Jack's focus back to his life purpose, his soul brought about the fall that caused his paralysis.

Although this means of steering Jack's plan may seem drastic, his soul had other motives for this choice. Jack had become callous and impatient toward those who couldn't perform as well athletically. He didn't realize that his athletic talent came from lifetimes of development that others didn't have. The paralysis balanced this callousness and developed his compassion.

If Jack's soul had felt that its goals couldn't be accomplished this way, other tactics would've been used or that particular life purpose abandoned and replaced by one related to his physical skills. The soul has many options, and it often does alter the life plan in midstream, in small and larger ways. But, knowing that Jack had the inner strength and astrology chart to support mental accomplishments, not just physical ones, his soul chose this plan.

Case I

Barry sustained a brain injury when he fell from a window. The trauma left him temporarily unable to speak or write, although he could understand what was said to him. This accident had been planned before life to accomplish two things. First, it would give Barry an opportunity to develop patient, focused perseverance. In previous lifetimes, he'd gotten into the habit of not finishing what he started, which prevented him from developing his talents and certain virtues, such as patience, hard work, and endurance. Second, it would give Barry an opportunity to develop his inner life, which he'd avoided in previous lifetimes. He was someone who was always on the go, moving from one activity to the next, with little direction or thought given to the value of those activities in his life.

During his recovery, Barry had hour after hour to contemplate his predicament, to wonder, and to be still and listen. His condition forced him to become an observer of life. Now, as someone on the sidelines of life, he contemplated human nature and the human drama around him. He also began to recognize an aspect of himself that was beyond this drama, an aspect beyond his personality, body, emotions, or mind. This was the greatest gift of his disability, a rare treasure that few experience except in their last incarnations.

Accidents that aren't part of the soul's plan are rare because the soul can often waylay them or minimize their effects. By working through the intuition and even by speaking directly to you, your soul can influence your choices, such as how quickly you turn, what direction you turn, and other responses that you or others might make in a critical situation. So, it's usually not by chance that some people walk away from disasters while others don't. This doesn't mean that those who are injured or die deserve this for some reason. Injury or death is never a punishment. It merely suits or doesn't suit the soul's plan at that time.

Murder and Suicide

Taking someone's life is a most grievous offense. When someone's life is lost, so are many opportunities. Killing someone interferes with free will in the most extreme way possible. It interrupts the soul's plan, making it necessary for that soul to begin life again and bypass other goals in order to heal.

If it were possible to relive that life again, the loss might not be so great, but it never is. Those same circumstances can never be duplicated. The victim may have to wait many lifetimes before similar opportunities present themselves again. This is also true of suicide.

Killing also sets the murderer back. The murderer will be required to make reparations to the victim and experience whatever's necessary to prevent the murderer from killing again. Karma encompasses both learning and atonement, which can be made in many different ways besides directly to the victim.

Suicide and murder require different lessons and, consequently, different strategies for healing, or balancing. Suicide slows one's evolution, although the soul even learns from this. Fortunately, because the fruitlessness of suicide is apparent once the person is out of the body and the memory of its fruitlessness persists on a deep level when reincarnated, that person rarely commits suicide again.

Every human being has committed suicide because it's a

natural response to the pain experienced in your earliest lifetimes, when you have few resources for dealing with life. Lately, suicide has become common in teenagers, who may be older souls but lack the maturity for coping with life and who may have fallen under negative influences. Certain drugs have also played a part in suicide among some older souls.

The stories that follow show how killing and being killed are healed and how a soul grows in love and compassion as a result.

Murder

Case J

Arnold committed murder in one of his earliest incarnations. Most murders and suicides happen early in the soul's evolution, before the compassion, understanding, and self-control to inhibit them have been developed. When older souls commit murder, it's often a reaction to violence and hatred they experienced in their childhood.

Arnold grew up in a normal family for the times and, although he wasn't treated harshly or neglected, life was hard. He worked in the fields from sunup to sundown. Lacking the discipline or physical strength to manage this without resentment and anger, Arnold coped by drinking, which lowered his inhibitions and unleashed his anger. As a consequence, he often got into fights with others who were also acting out. One day, a fistfight turned into a knife fight, and Arnold's opponent lost his life. Due to a lack of law enforcement, Arnold's crime went unpunished, and so his behavior never changed.

In his next lifetime, he reincarnated as a female named Ellen. Ellen worked in the fields in addition to caring for her invalid parents, her husband, and her children. This was another lifetime of hard work with little reward, but being a female, she wasn't allowed to express her anger. She found other ways of dealing with her feelings, such as talking with others, which relieved her of feeling persecuted and helped her accept her lot in life. She also learned to find pleasure in some of her daily tasks, especially sewing, weaving, and knitting. She discovered she could make lovely clothing, which gave her a sense of fulfillment and pride.

Ellen's soul chose this situation for two reasons. First, it gave her a chance to face circumstances similar to those in her former life and improve her way of dealing with them. Second, although neither her mother nor her father was her former victim, caring for them was a way of partially repaying the karmic debt from that lifetime. To make it easier, her soul chose warm and generous parents. This way, it was almost assured that Ellen would work off some of the debt as well as increase her ability to love and serve others.

For her next lifetime, her soul chose happier circumstances, again as a female. The goal was to continue to strengthen her capacity to love. For this, she needed to experience the goodness of life. She was born to a warm, loving family dedicated to the ministry. Her parents raised money for the poor, fed and sheltered the homeless, gave of themselves to their parishioners, and still had plenty of love left over for their three children.

Although she wasn't as evolved as her other siblings, her good qualities were brought out and enhanced by the loving people around her. Her beauty also made her more lovable. When it came time for her to marry, she chose someone with the same calling as her father's, which continued the pattern of service. During this lifetime, she grew in inner strength, love, and understanding.

Over these lifetimes, she became strong enough for the final test. At last, as a male, she would meet the individual she'd killed and try to make final amends. Although people aren't required to meet again in another lifetime to balance karmic debts like this one, many choose to. This will only be allowed if the victim consents to it, however. The victim has to be careful in making this choice because it's never certain that a balancing will go as planned.

Let's backtrack a moment and chart the victim's course. If you recall, the victim had a problem with anger too. To correct this, several female lifetimes were chosen, as they were for the offender. One of these was a lifetime of ease, which allowed her to develop a talent and other resources. As we saw in the offender's story, a talent (making clothing) was useful in her healing as well. The soul often uses someone's talents to overcome his or her challenges. This is one reason people evolve more quickly in their later incarnations, when they have more talents, than in their earlier ones, when they have fewer.

At last, the victim, Rose, and the offender, Jim, met. They fell in love at first sight at a dance. Soon after that, they were married. Although this may seem inconceivable, many marriages and other relationships are founded on a karmic debt. The souls of the individuals bring them together under the guise of romantic love and bind them until the debt is met or met as much as the circumstances allow. Although either individual could leave anytime, karma causes them to feel a sense of obligation, compulsion, attraction, and sometimes repulsion. To those involved in a karmic relationship, it often feels like being under a spell.

To continue, before long, Rose fell deathly ill. The test had arrived. Would Jim care for her in her hour of need? Was he a loving enough person to do that? Favoring this was the sense of obligation that is felt from a karmic debt, which fosters love and commitment between two people. Through your karmic relationships, you learn the meaning of commitment, and your ability to love is strengthened through that commitment. This was true for Rose and Jim. Jim nurtured Rose unwaveringly until she recovered, and although they were no longer obligated to remain together for karmic reasons, they gladly did.

This story is not unusual; many soulmate relationships begin as karmic relationships. This story shows how even murder can lead to love. In case you haven't already guessed, love is the outcome of all of life's stories and the outcome of the next one too.

Case K

This is another story of murder. It took place in the earlier incarnations of both involved. Sam, who took Henry's life, did it out of fear because Henry was threatening him with a weapon. This brings up some interesting questions. Just as laws make some allowances for killing under these circumstances, the soul might also be expected to. From the standpoint of atonement, this murder would require less atonement than some. But from the soul's standpoint, the question isn't how heinous a crime is but what lack of understanding caused it and what lessons are needed to correct it. To answer these questions, we need to look more closely at what happened and why.

Sam and Henry knew each other and considered themselves friends. Their disagreement was over some livestock that Sam presumably owed Henry. When Henry came to claim what he believed was his, Sam met his hostility with more of the same. A fight ensued and Henry was killed.

From their souls' perspective, their feelings when this happened are crucial. Sam had his wife and two children in mind when he defended himself. Although Sam had responded aggressively, it wasn't out of rage, as Henry had. So, Sam's lesson wouldn't be about controlling his anger. Still, Sam had ended someone's life, so he needed to be impressed with the sanctity of life.

Sam chose to learn this dramatically by having his next lifetime cut short. He could have chosen a gentler but slower way to do this, but this way had its benefits. When that lifetime ended so abruptly, it was a great loss to everyone who loved him, even though this was part of his loved ones' plans too. Loss brings with it many opportunities for growth for everyone touched by it. The lesson being complete, he entered his next lifetime with more compassion and a contagious appreciation for life.

Suicide

Suicide happens for many reasons. Why it occurred is important in determining the lesson that will follow it. There are several reasons for suicide, among them are being overcome by feelings of hopelessness and other negativity, inadequate coping mechanisms and resources, fear of the future, and to escape from physical pain. Suicide also happens because people lack spiritual understanding, particularly about the soul and reincarnation. If people had more understanding of life and death, suicide wouldn't be seen as an option.

One way the soul teaches people about life and death is through near-death experiences. People return from these experiences with an awareness of their own vastness and immortality and a greater understanding of the purpose of life — and they share this understanding with others, at least these days. Following a near-death experience, life becomes more than a search for happiness; it is seen as a gift whose value is deepened by every experience — even painful ones.

Near-death experiences are an antidote to suicide, but there are others. Religion is one. Young souls who are vulnerable to thoughts of suicide are often born into religious families. By discouraging suicide, religions encourage facing life. Some religions even teach that life is a school, but few religions provide an understanding that helps people embrace and cope with life no matter what life brings. Understanding is a basic human need. It counteracts the ego's hopelessness and fear and fosters acceptance and compassion. Understanding is the best antidote to suicide. This is illustrated by the next story.

Case L

Anna began her life in a prison. Her mother was incarcerated for a theft she didn't commit. At age two, Anna was placed with a foster family outside the prison walls in the hope that she would grow up normally. Those who raised her took good care of her, but no one offered her any spiritual understanding. No one taught her that there's more to life and to herself than the obvious. Although life may not depend on this understanding, the quality of life does.

As a result, Anna grew up with little sense of herself beyond whatever currently held her attention. Living without any spiritual understanding is like living with blinders on: You miss the big picture. This was true for Anna. When faced with a problem, her context for understanding it was so narrow that she couldn't see her options or the problem's potential for good. So, out of desperation and ignorance, she took her own life.

For her next lifetime, Anna's soul devised a plan that would introduce her spiritual nature to her. A religious family was chosen along with an astrology chart that encouraged a search for higher meaning (Sagittarius and Pisces). She was born to a devout family that believed that God resides within everyone.

Her first experience of her spiritual self wouldn't be an earth-shattering or transcendent one. Instead, awareness of this grew slowly within her until one day she was struck by feelings of devotion. Next, she became aware of a peaceful place within herself. Having made these two important discoveries, she was on her way to accomplishing her life purpose. But there was more.

One day, while waiting on a street corner for a ride, her vision shifted and she saw that all life was connected. She saw energy streaming out of and connected to every other form. This lasted only a brief second, but it would remain with her the rest of her life. In that brief moment, she knew that life was not as it seemed. She knew that behind ordinary reality was a far different one. And she knew that she was inseparable from the rest of life. For her, this was the birth of that mysterious thing called faith.

Experiences like these are given to each of you by your soul at various points in your evolution to bring about similar realizations. They form the basis of what is known as faith. When she encountered difficulties in her next lifetime, she didn't consider suicide. Instead, she found that she had an inner strength—faith—that she could draw on to help her persevere and learn from her difficulties.

Case M

Betty, a young soul, had difficulty coping with even life's littlest challenges, such as getting up in the morning, fulfilling responsibilities, communicating needs, and getting along with family members. She attributed this to being different and assumed this meant she was special. Feeling special helped her cope with her daily difficulties. When she felt persecuted or unloved, she'd withdraw to her room and tell herself she was above it all. She indulged in elaborate fantasies about what her life would be like in the future.

As Betty matured, little changed. When she began working as a clerk in her father's store, she approached it like everything else. She arrived at work late and treated the customers badly. When she was reprimanded, she didn't care. She continued to believe that she was special and destined for something greater and dreamed of a husband who would take her away from the drudgery of her life and provide for her every need. She didn't understand that her choices create her future, not her fantasies.

One day, Betty met the man of her dreams, or so she thought. She flirted with him, and he asked her for a date. Their evening together was romantic, he was mysterious, and she was completely charmed. They continued to see each other until, one day, he told her that he couldn't see her anymore because he was married. She was crushed. He was perfect for her! How could this happen to her! That night, she went home, took a knife to her wrist, and bled to death.

If she'd had more resources for dealing with this blow and not so much invested in fantasy with this man, she might have been able to grow from this experience. Several conclusions other than the one she chose were possible. She might have concluded that she couldn't count on others to improve her life and that she had to improve herself to attract the right man. Instead, she concluded that life wasn't worth living without this man.

In designing a plan for her next lifetime, Betty's soul considered the conclusion she'd come to that caused her suicide and her level of spiritual development. This plan included circumstances that would encourage her to develop a talent, parents whose religious convictions prohibited suicide, and an astrology chart that would limit fantasy and promote realism and hard work (earth signs). Correcting her ill-conceived conclusion at death demanded a slightly more creative approach. Because she'd concluded that life wasn't worth living without this man, her soul would try to arrange a marriage to the man of her dreams so that she'd see that wasn't the answer.

As expected, she was more practical in this lifetime. She took care of her responsibilities more willingly, but not without some resentment. This isn't surprising. Even though an astrology chart brings out certain tendencies, it can't make up for a lack of spiritual development.

As planned, she met, fell in love with, and married the man of her dreams. But not long after that, he started drinking and staying out all night. Sometimes he'd come home in a drunken stupor, wake her up, and beat her. After one of these nights, she decided that she'd had enough and left him.

This opened up new avenues for her. An elderly couple who wanted to share their home with someone in exchange for household tasks took her in. This made it possible for her to study art, an interest she'd wanted to pursue since she was a child. She did this while supporting herself with other kinds of jobs. Her self-sufficiency and the freedom to pursue her own interests made this lifetime a very fulfilling one.

It should be apparent from these stories that karma isn't about punishment. How painful it is to learn a particular lesson isn't necessarily equal to the severity of a crime. This doesn't mean that someone who kills thousands of people won't suffer for it. The greater the transgression, the greater the atonement, and both learning and atonement often involve suffering. Furthermore, one's evolutionary progress is slowed significantly by having to make amends, and having to live more lifetimes is punishment of a sort. But the most difficult aspect of karma may be the need to postpone progress in other areas. Lifetimes dedicated to karmic debts are rarely as fulfilling as those dedicated to other goals.

Unfortunate Love Affairs

When a love affair turns out painfully, it can affect later relationships, including those in future lifetimes if the wounds are deep enough. Wounds deep enough to leave emotional scars lasting into other lifetimes are usually those in which abandonment, a loveless marriage, or infidelity has led to injury or death. This section examines how these experiences can be healed and their karma balanced.

Abandonment

Case N

Juan and Maria married shortly after they met and immediately began a family. As can be expected, providing for their three young children was very stressful. Juan worked long hours, while Maria cared for the children. One day, Juan didn't come home. He returned the next day, without speaking, only to pick up some of his belongings. His father had abandoned his mother when he was a child, and now he was repeating the pattern. He probably never should have married or had children. It was contrary to his astrology chart, which was another reason he was so unhappy, although this is no excuse.

Abandonment is a serious offense, requiring atonement if it causes suffering. Mistakes like this are common with younger souls, who often fall out of alignment with their soul's plan. When that happens, the soul can usually improvise another plan. If Juan had remained with Maria, it would have been difficult, but he would have grown. Instead, he was led to a more satisfying life, one more in keeping with his plan, but he still incurred a karmic debt to those he'd abandoned.

Abandonment requires atonement when it causes hardship, as it did for Juan's wife and children. His children concluded that they weren't lovable, and Maria concluded she wasn't attractive or womanly enough to keep her husband. Although she never expressed these feelings, they kept her from pursuing another relationship. She concentrated on raising her children and being the best person she could be under the circumstances. Without a husband to support her, her life was very difficult.

In her next lifetime, it was important for her to get involved in relationships again so that her growth wouldn't be stunted by avoiding them. For this, her soul chose an attractive appearance and an astrology chart that would increase her confidence and ensure opportunities for love. Her soul also arranged a meeting with someone she'd loved in a former lifetime with the intention that they would fall in love again.

Standing on the sidelines of love will never mend a broken heart. So, when trust is an issue, the soul will make it as easy as possible to open up to love again. When she first met the man she had loved in another lifetime, she had reservations. She didn't trust him even though she had no reason not to. Eventually, his patience and their former love overcame her inhibitions.

The next story has a different ending. Sometimes the soul makes finding and maintaining a relationship difficult.

Case O

This story begins like the last, with a broken marriage and abandoned children. Like the husband in the last story, Thomas found the responsibilities of married life unbearable. He left because he wasn't able to support his wife and children and because he dreaded being tied down to a job. So, Thomas took off

Karmic Justice and Healing Traumas

with a goal of seeing the world and making money as he needed it. With no particular plan in mind, he let circumstances determine his course. When he met someone who needed a hand on a ship headed for another continent, he joined on.

Thomas hadn't gone far before he realized he'd made a mistake. He missed the comfort of his wife, Milly, and the smiling faces of their two children. He couldn't get them out of his mind and vowed to return to them as soon as he could. Unfortunately, that wouldn't be for months, and he couldn't get a message to them either. At least this gave him plenty of time to think about what he'd done.

When he arrived home, he was coolly received. During Thomas's absence, Milly had moved in with her parents, where she was supporting herself and her children by taking in laundry. Moreover, she had a new love and wanted nothing to do with Thomas.

He was deeply hurt by this and determined to win her and his children back. One night while everyone was asleep, he stole into her room and tried to convince her to take him back. Her parents woke up and came in to see what the noise was all about. They chased Thomas out and threatened to have him arrested.

This didn't stop him. He continued intruding on her in futile attempts to win her affection. Finally, she'd had enough and summoned the police, who jailed him for a short time. That only made Thomas more determined to have his wife or prevent anyone else from having her. In his desperation, he killed her and spent the remainder of his life behind bars.

In his next lifetime, he was born with a facial deformity, which inhibited his chances for romance. This challenge was intended to teach him the value of relationships (not having one is one way of doing this). He spent this lifetime reading and helping other outcasts. He especially enjoyed his time at an orphanage, where he would hold the babies and play games with the older children. These children became his family, and his work with them enabled him to balance some of his karma.

In his next lifetime, he was the grandfather of the individual who'd been his wife. When he died, he left her a large sum of money. For several lifetimes following that one, he continued to donate time and money to helping children until his debt was fully paid. As a result, his compassion, love, and desire to serve grew.

Loveless Marriages

Loveless marriages exist for many reasons, mostly for convenience, security, or raising children. Some are arranged and some are the result of poor choices or karma. Loveless marriages are most common when religious or philosophical beliefs prohibit divorce or separation. Significant psychological and even physical injury can result from a loveless marriage if anger and resentment escalate toward hatred or violence.

Relationships serve many purposes for the soul, some of which can be fulfilled within a short period of time. Consequently, divorce may serve the soul's plan more than staying together does. When that's the case, religious beliefs that prohibit divorce work against the highest good of those involved.

On the other hand, prohibition of divorce is helpful when commitment and love are being learned or when karma is being balanced. Nevertheless, when commitment is forced, it can turn to anger and resentment. The value of commitment isn't taught by forcing people to stay together but through loving interactions. When people feel forced to stay together, marriages can become boiling pots of hatred and resentment. If this happens, the individuals may have to meet again in future lifetimes.

Case P

Sanjay and Roma married because their families arranged it. Although some arranged marriages are happy, this one wasn't. Roma wasn't attracted to her husband, who was nearly fifteen years her senior. Furthermore, Sanjay didn't understand her needs or see her as anything more than a possession. Although he was attracted to her and found her pleasant to be with, Sanjay and Roma didn't have enough in common to have anything more than a marriage of convenience. As a result, Sanjay had liaisons with other women, which satisfied some of his other needs. But this wasn't an option for Roma. She felt her only recourse was death, since religious law forbade divorce. She chose suicide rather than stay in that marriage.

Roma reincarnated at a time and place where arranged marriages were a matter of course because those circumstances could further her lessons. The arranged marriage was part of her soul's plan. She had known her husband in a former lifetime and had had difficulty with him then. They chose before life to be together to learn to love and support each other in a committed relationship. The potential for deeper love existed, but they weren't able to open their hearts to each other. With time, they might have succeeded.

In another life, Roma's soul chose to try again to love this same individual, which would also give him another chance to learn to love her. It took nearly a century before an opportunity arose for them to be together again. This time, their souls made a loving relationship more likely by arranging for them to be brother and sister. This worked, and they had a satisfying relationship, and they went on to further their love in the following lifetime as husband and wife.

The point is not that there should be arranged marriages, but that arranged marriages may serve to develop love for those who've avoided or ended relationships rather than persevered. This doesn't make arranged marriages right; they interfere with free will. But since they exist in your world, the soul may use them to bring about one's lessons.

Case Q

Mukunda and Uma also had an arranged marriage, but one for the purpose of developing talents, not love. Unlike the previous couple, Mukunda's and Uma's lack of engagement with each other was useful to their growth. Their marriage provided Uma with financial support and time to develop her musical abilities and Mukunda with an opportunity to repay a karmic debt he owed to her. The arranged marriage served both of them for that lifetime, resulting in a satisfying partnership.

A loveless marriage doesn't have to end in bad feelings or injury. Sometimes these situations accommodate the needs of both souls. Whether a loveless marriage or infidelity leads to psychological damage or not depends on the choices of those involved. The next story illustrates how infidelity can lead to karmic consequences. The story following that one illustrates a different outcome.

Infidelity

Case R

George and Amanda fell in love in their youth. As is usual with young love, neither understood themselves or their needs, but they married and began a family anyway. Before long, George became restless, feeling that something was missing in his life and that his wife and children were to blame.

One day, without warning, George disappeared for a few days. He wanted to get away from his daily grind and be alone. Instead, he ran into some single friends who convinced him to go to a brothel with them.

When he returned home, George told Amanda that he'd discovered that the single life wasn't for him, which was true. Unfortunately, Amanda didn't believe him and began to feel insecure. She'd been betrayed in former lifetimes, so it wasn't surprising she felt distrustful despite his reassurances.

Amanda began looking through George's things and questioning his whereabouts. She also questioned her own attractiveness. One night she went out, presumably with friends, but ended up in a tavern where she met a man. They began meeting regularly and began an affair. When George followed Amanda one night and discovered her secret, he confronted her lover and they fought. Before anyone realized what was happening, George had delivered a deadly blow to his rival's head.

Needless to say, George would have to pay in this lifetime and several to come for not controlling his jealous temper. Amanda also suffered, for her lover's blood was on her hands too. She also lost a husband to provide for her and her children. This was a high price to pay for her indiscretion. Still, she needed more to ensure that this wouldn't happen again.

In her next lifetime she was raised in a small village where marriages were arranged and monogamy was the rule. This way of life wasn't questioned, and everyone made the best of the situation. She learned to do this too. Because infidelity wasn't tolerated, she no longer feared it and she learned to focus on values other than sexual attractiveness.

George had different lessons. First, he needed to learn to handle his jealousy and anger. Second, he needed to make atonement to the man he'd killed. And third, he needed to learn the value of commitment.

To achieve these goals, his soul chose to be born into a wealthy and respectable family. His good fortune allowed him to act as a benefactor to the man he'd killed (which only partially atoned for this), and his upbringing taught him to handle his feelings in a socially acceptable way.

His soul also arranged for him to fall in love with a religious woman, who was likely to remain faithful to him. This environment reduced the likelihood that anger and jealousy would be a problem because it lacked the frustrations common to poverty and provided the social constraints and values needed for a committed relationship.

It may seem odd that George's lessons were taught without pain or sacrifice. People are used to thinking of karma as punishment. The problem with looking at karma this way is that you might assume that those who are suffering deserve it because of something they did. This story shows the fallacy of this. As many saints have chosen challenging circumstances as sinners, and as many sinners are successful by society's standards as saints.

Case S

Brad and Carolyn knew each other in a former lifetime. In that lifetime, Brad had harmed Carolyn. In this one, he'd try to balance this karmic debt. The plan was simple: Brad would be born to a wealthy family, and Brad and Carolyn would fall in love and marry. This way, Brad would have the opportunity to repay Carolyn by supporting her in a comfortable lifestyle.

Brad and Carolyn married and lived comfortably for the first few years. Then, an unexpected misfortune hit the family, causing them to lose most of their money. After this, one bad financial decision after another compounded the stress on their marriage. Brad and Carolyn continued to grow apart as bitterness over their situation grew, each blaming the other for their problems.

Then, one day, Carolyn spent a seemingly innocent afternoon with a male friend, to whom she confided her troubles. They fell in love unexpectedly. Carolyn told Brad she was in love with another man and left Brad to be with him. Before long, Carolyn realized what she really wanted wasn't another marriage but time to discover who she was.

In this case, infidelity served a purpose. This couple had moved out of alignment with their plans, and the karmic debt owed to the wife couldn't be balanced under these new circumstances. Infidelity was the tool the soul used to end the karmic agreement and set both on new courses.

Unfulfilled Potential

Many lead unfulfilling lives. An unfulfilling lifetime can affect future lifetimes in several ways. For one, it can result in confusion about what you want, which can lead to another unfulfilling lifetime. If that happens, the soul will probably choose an astrology chart to try to break this cycle. A chart with a strong theme might be chosen, such as one with many planets in the same sign. Such a chart narrows one's focus and concentrates one's energy, since the tendencies of that sign are difficult to ignore. Or, because significant people in one's life have such a powerful influence on one's attitudes and behavior, the soul might arrange for someone to offer guidance or model decisiveness and initiative.

The most common result of having several unfulfilling lifetimes is the belief that life is drudgery, which can become a self-fulfilling prophecy, leading to more unsatisfactory lifetimes. If you expect drudgery, you aren't likely to seek joy and fulfillment. And that's unfortunate because following your joy is how you align with your soul's plan and find fulfillment.

Even though every life has some drudgery, if you're aligned with your soul's plan, you'll feel enlivened and excited about what lies ahead. A lack of fulfillment is nearly always a lack of alignment with the soul's plan.

The soul also conveys its plan through the intuition, so learning to listen to and follow your intuition is necessary for fulfillment. This isn't always easy, however, because the voice in your head is captivating, and the intuition is more subtle than that.

It takes many, many lifetimes of trial and error to learn to use the intuition. It also takes many lifetimes to learn how to find fulfillment. Ironically, but not surprisingly, this is first learned by experiencing a lack of fulfillment. This lack of fulfillment leads to questioning what you're allowing to guide you—in failing, you learn to succeed.

This paradox exists because the physical plane is a plane of polarities, which means that you learn about something by experiencing its opposite. You know what light is because you've experienced dark; you know joy because you've experienced pain. Consequently, no lifetime—even an unfulfilling one—is ever wasted.

Unfulfilled potentials can also cause people to distrust life and themselves in future lifetimes, resulting in bitterness and fatalism. When you're out of alignment with your soul's plan, life is more difficult because your soul will keep trying to bring you back to your plan, sometimes in ways that are unpleasant. If you keep missing your soul's messages, more extreme methods will be used to get your attention.

Physical illness is just one way the soul redirects people from one thing to another. Another way is to introduce change, such as loss of employment, difficulties with a child or spouse, or financial loss. Life always has its challenges, but they will be fewer if you're tuned in to your soul's plan. So, the remedy for bitterness and fatalism is to become more aligned with your plan.

Many unfulfilled people find their way to therapists or healers, where they learn to get in touch with their feelings. This is often helpful because the soul uses feelings to guide you, at least some of them. Feelings of depression, anger, sadness, and hopelessness often indicate that your needs—including your soul's needs—aren't being met, while joy points you in a direction aligned with your soul.

Case T

Lucy was a slave for a family that had little concern for her as a human being. Because she had no freedom to make choices then, she didn't learn to make them. She was told what to do and when and how to do it. This childlike position kept her from developing the skills of an independent adult. So, not only did Lucy have an unfulfilling life then, but she also didn't develop skills that would be helpful in future lifetimes.

To counteract the effects of this experience, her soul chose a male incarnation next and an astrology chart and environment that would foster independence and initiative. Still, taking initiative didn't come easily to him, although he eventually got better at this and became a successful businessman. This lifetime helped to balance the deficiencies of his lifetime as a slave, but the story doesn't end here.

In his next lifetime, he was born into a family dedicated to ending slavery. The plan was that he, now named Ben, would use the assertiveness and initiative he'd developed since his lifetime as a slave to further his family's cause. But life doesn't always go as planned. Ben felt uncomfortable with the issue of ending slavery, so he immersed himself in his business, even though this wasn't particularly fulfilling.

Ben's soul had to find a way to draw out his compassion so that it could be used to fuel his life purpose. It did this by bringing a woman into his life whom he'd loved in his lifetime as a slave. As his heart opened to her, he discovered his own sensitivity. His love for her activated his latent compassion and passion for the cause of slavery, which was also a passion of hers.

Case U

This story is different. It's about someone who tried to find fulfillment but couldn't. Like many people, he believed that fulfillment could be found in eating, drinking, and sex. He spent his life pursuing these pleasures, but in the end, he still felt empty and dissatisfied and died an unhappy, addicted man.

In his next lifetime, he still believed that happiness and fulfillment could be found by pursuing the ego's desires. But in this lifetime, he indulged in different things. He concentrated on amassing material possessions and creating a comfortable lifestyle. Once again, he died feeling empty and unfulfilled.

In his next lifetime, he tried another tactic. This time, he denounced the ego's desires and turned to the priesthood in search of fulfillment. In serving others as a priest, he experienced more fulfillment and happiness than he ever had before. So, for his next lifetime, he chose an astrology chart and environment that would deepen his ability to serve.

This series of lifetimes illustrates how the soul often allows a natural course of learning to take place. The soul honors free will, as it did in this story by allowing this individual to pursue his concept of fulfillment until he learned to choose more wisely.

This story is a reminder that fulfillment may be found only after many lifetimes without it. Fulfillment is usually found as a matter of course unless the vicious cycle mentioned earlier comes into play. If that happens, the soul may have to intervene. Although this cycle can usually be broken by selecting the right astrology chart and environment, sometimes more drastic measures are necessary. The next story describes such an instance.

Case V

This story begins with a lifetime of poverty and oppression. Every human being experiences financial limitation at times in the course of one's evolution because it teaches certain lessons, but poverty can also simply be caused by one's choices. Lifetimes of financial limitation often lead to unfulfilling lifetimes because the oppression of poverty squelches the human spirit.

When this happens, a sense of resignation and powerlessness might follow someone from one lifetime to the next until something intervenes. That's what happened to this individual. Feelings of resignation and powerlessness followed him into his next lifetime and then into another before the soul made choices to correct this.

This issue was finally addressed by choosing an assertive and ambitious astrology chart and an environment that allowed him freedom. This time, he was born into a white family in the United States in recent years. If that family had been black much before today, his feelings of powerlessness and resignation would probably have been culturally reinforced. But nothing in his environment gave him the message that he couldn't create the kind of life he wanted.

What happened was unexpected, however. Rather than behaving confidently and assertively, he continued to act as if he were oppressed and limited. Sometimes the chart and environment are just not enough to counteract the influence of many lifetimes.

To correct this, his soul arranged that he win a large sum of money. Since money is equated with power in American culture, this gave him the confidence he needed. It also gave him the opportunity to develop his athletic skills, which furthered his self-confidence and sense of mastery. As he matured, he achieved other goals, which continued to reinforce his sense of power and control. If he'd failed in these endeavors, his soul might have introduced other means to build his confidence. So, sometimes the soul brings good fortune into people's lives regardless of merit if it serves their growth, as it did in this instance.

Slavery and Servitude

Sometime in the course of the soul's evolution, usually in the earlier lifetimes, slavery and servitude must be experienced. These experiences are a necessary part of the soul's evolution because they teach compassion, loyalty, humility, selfless giving, and the importance of human rights. In fact, many who in their later lifetimes pursue life purposes involving service have often had numerous lifetimes of slavery or servitude, which developed their compassion and altruism. However, just because slavery serves an evolutionary purpose doesn't excuse it. The oppressor must, at some point, come to realize the damage caused by inhibiting another's freedom.

Although slavery and oppression teach valuable lessons,

these experiences are damaging psychologically. They affect how people see themselves in relation to others. Those who've had many lifetimes of slavery or servitude often feel inferior and form relationships that reinforce this. Their tendency to be subservient results in them giving too much or giving inappropriately to others.

The experience of slavery can also result in feelings of powerlessness and hopelessness, which can attract further oppression, poverty, and servitude in subsequent lifetimes, thus creating a vicious cycle. In later lifetimes, the oppressor is internalized and restrictions are created, not by an outsider, but by one's own limiting beliefs. Often, the soul has to intervene to break the cycle created by the repetition of these experiences. Slavery and servitude are combined in this section, not because they are the same, but because lifetimes of servitude often follow lifetimes of slavery.

Case W

This is the story of someone who had several lifetimes as a slave and a servant. When it came time to serve in less subservient ways, low self-esteem, the result of his earlier experiences, interfered with feeling fulfilled in his work. The more he gave, the worse he felt about himself. For him to serve more joyfully, this would have to change.

The circumstances his soul chose to build self-esteem were what you might expect: He was born into a wealthy and powerful family. Although he was somewhat uncomfortable with the power he had, this lifetime built his self-esteem, clarified the meaning of service for him, and showed him he was capable of leadership.

These arrangements don't always work out so neatly,

however. Sometimes those who've been servants for many lifetimes don't overcome their sense of inferiority so easily. When this happens, their evolution is slowed while time is taken to balance this. Some may even decide to pursue other avenues of growth instead of returning to the path of service. Regardless, these initial lifetimes of service teach many valuable lessons.

Let's go back and see what was learned from this individual's experiences with slavery. In his first lifetime as a slave, he was treated badly by his owner. He was bought to do hard physical labor, and his master was determined to get his money's worth. However, even though he was treated like an animal, he knew better. To him, this cruelty proved his master, not himself, to be the animal—or worse. Despite this harsh treatment, he retained his sense of pride and learned that social class isn't the measure of a human being.

In his next lifetime, he chose slavery again, with a goal of helping other slaves retain their pride amidst their oppression. He was able to serve as a model for this because of his astrology chart and two previous lifetimes of mental illness, which developed his compassion and understanding.

Other experiences of servitude continued to build his compassion and understanding. These lifetimes also motivated him to serve, not a master, but as a teacher for the oppressed. Serving an ungrateful and cruel master doesn't increase one's desire to serve, but it can build one's compassion to the point that humanitarian service becomes compelling.

The next story of slavery is different because the girl in this story didn't have the same degree of understanding to bring to her experience of slavery. The first experience of slavery usually occurs in early lifetimes when the lessons of slavery are most pertinent and before one has much understanding. Slavery provides a vehicle for learning some of the most basic human lessons, such as learning to work hard, follow instructions, perseverance, diligence, humility, caution, patience, and fortitude. Many older souls also choose slavery for their own reasons, as another story will show.

When young souls experience slavery, their initial reaction is usually to agree with their oppressor's assessment of them. Just as children take a parent's word for who they are and what they can do, younger souls believe what others say about them. Realizing you aren't inferior is a big step in mastering the lessons of slavery. This realization may come during the first experience of slavery or several lifetimes of slavery later. When it does come, it signals one's readiness to move beyond this experience if one chooses to. As we saw in the last story, some choose to remain slaves for a time to either help the enslaved or heighten their own compassion and drive to serve. The next story describes what most people experience before they're ready to move on to other lessons.

Case X

Karinna was born into conditions of slavery. Although she lived with her family, her interactions with her parents were limited by their exhaustion from working such long hours. Her parents would take her along with them into the fields where she would occupy herself with whatever was available. She grew up this way, having little experience with the world or how others lived. She never saw the more luxurious homes of the wealthy because the rich lived some distance from their small enclave of huts, although she heard stories of their comforts and wealth.

When the overseers came to collect the little that Karinna's community had to show for their labors, the laborers were verbally abused and spat on. It didn't take long before Karinna began to believe that she and her family were being punished for being who they were. Clearly, some people were favored over others, and her religious beliefs led her to believe that the fortunate were better people than the unfortunate.

Her family didn't contradict these ideas with assertions of injustice or criticism of the wealthy. Rather, they looked to their oppressors as gods who had the power to bestow happiness on them if they proved themselves worthy. This attitude isn't typical of all slaves, but it is typical of younger souls caught in slavery.

One day, a man appeared on horseback. He had come some distance to deliver a proclamation. It stated that Karinna's community was no longer bound to a certain individual but to someone else. As a result, they would have to hand over a larger portion of their produce than before.

Needless to say, this was a great hardship for their community. Some of the younger men talked of protesting by holding back some of what was due, but what would that mean? For one, it would mean they were worthy of making a decision like this, an idea unacceptable to some. After all, who were they to question their rulers?

Karinna had just become old enough to marry when this happened, and she had some ideas of her own. Her fear was that if her community rebelled, the strongest and bravest of her small community would have to answer for it. She didn't want to see anyone hurt. She'd suffered all her life and she would suffer some more, but the disruption of her community was more than she was willing to risk. However, her opinion mattered little and her worst fears came to pass. The man she most wanted to marry was taken and jailed. Karinna died several years later, ending this hard, lonely life.

In another lifetime, she reincarnated as a male slave named Harvey, who worked in the stables of a wealthy landowner.

Harvey was reliable, trustworthy, and content. He had no desire to improve his lot in life nor did he see any opportunity to. Then, one day, another stableman was taken on who had traveled the world with his former master. As they worked, Harvey heard tales of places he'd never even imagined existed and began to long for his freedom. The new stableman also told Harvey of an underground network where slaves could be taken safely to freedom. This gave rise to a plan, which won them the freedom they longed for.

Karinna's experience of slavery taught her some basic lessons. She learned to work hard and attend to responsibilities necessary to survival. The early lifetimes often revolve around survival. From the struggle with survival, patience, perseverance, and basic physical skills are learned. From humbling conditions, humility is learned. By being powerless, one learns to be receptive, accepting, and appreciative of the little things in life. Through service to others, one learns to be loyal, to obey, and to follow orders. These aren't minor accomplishments, although most people take them for granted. Because most people are no longer in their earliest incarnations, it may be hard to appreciate the importance of these lessons. Nevertheless, your current capabilities stem from these early lifetimes of struggle with survival.

By the next lifetime of slavery, as Harvey the stableman, he had sufficient mastery over these basic lessons to graduate from slavery once he realized the injustice of it, but he needed help coming to this realization. His previous experience of slavery, as Karinna, had taught him that rebellion wasn't wise when he, as Karinna, lost a lover to imprisonment for rebellion. To help Harvey break free of slavery, his soul arranged for him to meet an adventuresome, freedom-loving individual. If Harvey hadn't been ready to move beyond slavery, he probably wouldn't have met this liberator.

It would be naive to assume that this individual was unscathed by these experiences of slavery. It took several lifetimes with strong (fiery) astrology charts to overcome the passivity that had developed from these lifetimes of slavery. Charts and circumstances were also chosen to build relationship skills and eliminate subservient behavior. This individual had had little experience with intimate relationships before the two lifetimes of slavery, and those lifetimes were spent virtually alone. He needed practice forming equal partnerships.

Case Y

Unlike the last story, this one involves a very evolved soul who chose to experience slavery to advance his spiritual goals and improve the human condition. This individual had already experienced many lifetimes of slavery, servitude, and other forms of oppression, which had developed his appreciation of life and the preciousness of every human being.

As a result of these lifetimes, this individual learned to transform feelings of hatred, anger, resignation, and fear into compassion and understanding. He also developed an uncanny ability to intuit the feelings and inclinations of others. This may seem like an unlikely talent, but those who are oppressed learn to read their oppressors as a way of protecting themselves. They become astute observers of human nature and learn to manipulate it to ensure their safety.

This is one reason that those who've had many female lifetimes are sensitive and insightful. Sensitivity was an invaluable outgrowth of this individual's many lifetimes of oppression. Now he was prepared to enter into other oppressed circumstances, not to further his sensitivity, but to use his gifts for the good of all.

Around age eighteen, he was captured and taken on a boat to a faraway country. While traveling to this distant land, he was kept in shackles and fed a minimum of food until the food ran out. After that, he became very weak and unable to perform the work expected of him. He was beaten for his lack of productivity and left to mend.

In the delirium that followed, he had a vision of a distant and beautiful land, where rolling hills stretched for miles. He floated over this land, surveying it as if in flight, floating and gliding peacefully over its verdant valleys. Suddenly, he saw something that grabbed at his very being. There below him were people, like himself, laboring under the threat of a whip in the fields of this beautiful land. He saw himself among them, disheveled and stooped with exhaustion. At that moment a voice spoke to him saying, "Be at peace. Someday you will save your people from this oppression. When the time comes, you will be guided." From that point on, he began to recover from his fever despite not having had food for several more days.

As foretold, the next few years were filled with sweat and exhaustion, but he never forgot the powerful message of this vision. One day, as he lay on his mat on the floor, a figure of light appeared to him. It didn't speak, but it projected a mental picture of a rebellion with himself as its leader. Like a movie, it unfolded a plan for a rebellion in detail, showing him how he could lead others to freedom. It even indicated when this plan should be carried out. When the time came, he acted with the certainty and vision needed to inspire the confidence of others and lead them to freedom.

Although he suffered greatly in this lifetime, no healing was needed in future lifetimes. He was strong enough to live through this with no lingering psychological damage. This was not only because he was victorious, but because, throughout this trying experience, he knew he was more than a slave.

The vision had helped to crystallize his sense of purpose, but his many lifetimes had also taught him that great powers lay within him, and this gave him confidence that good would prevail. This set him apart from many of the others, but he's no more special than anyone else. He just had reached a point in his evolution, as everyone eventually does, when he was ready to give back to humanity what he'd learned from his many incarnations. Most of the world's greatest accomplishments have come from people like him who developed their talents, understanding, and desire to serve over many lifetimes of arduous lessons.

Mental Illness and Mental Disability

Mental illness and mental disability are being addressed in the same section because they often deliver similar lessons. But mental illness isn't always a pre-life choice and mental disability nearly always is. These conditions also evoke similar responses from others, with abuse being familiar to both.

Mental illness and mental disability have existed in every culture throughout history. Both are necessary to the soul's evolution because of what they have to teach both individuals and society. Compassion is the most obvious teaching but not the only one.

Just because most souls experience mental illness and mental disability in their early lifetimes doesn't mean that everyone who's mentally ill or mentally disabled is a young soul. Older souls choose these conditions too. Just as someone who's mastered the lessons of slavery might choose to experience slavery again to help those who are enslaved, many older souls choose mental illness or mental disability to help the afflicted make the best of this experience or to teach their caretakers important lessons.

You undoubtedly know or have heard of mentally ill or mentally disabled people who've taught their caretakers priceless lessons about love, compassion, acceptance, patience, and endurance. It's obvious that those who are mentally ill or mentally disabled aren't just learning lessons; they're also your teachers. These unusual people can enrich those who know them immensely.

The stories that follow illustrate how mental illness and mental disability can advance the soul's evolution and why these experiences are sometimes chosen by older souls.

Mental Illness

Case Z

Hanna suffered from schizophrenia in times when it was treated as possession. Because the townspeople thought Hanna was possessed by evil, she was feared and punished. Her soul chose this illness to accelerate her evolution, knowing that this choice at that place in time was likely to lead to abuse. Hanna was an older soul who was capable of using an experience of abuse for her growth, but the same might not have been true of a younger soul. For this reason, very young souls are rarely put in situations that are potentially abusive. Usually, when younger souls are abused, it's not part of their plan.

At first Hanna was jailed in unbearable conditions, but when it became a burden to continue to care for her, her oppressors found a way to justify her death. They said that, because she was a witch, she had to be burned to put an end to her sorcery. With great ceremony and self-righteousness, they burned her in the town square for all to see. This ended Hanna's life at the age of twenty.

Although this was a short life, it was a significant one. As all suffering does, it taught Hanna compassion. It also taught her to accept life and her lack of control of it. Her surrender gave rise to a new awareness, a new state of consciousness. As a result, in her next lifetime, she was able to remain detached from the ups and downs of life, centered amidst life's storms. She had learned what those who spend hours a day meditating learn—that she was not her body, her mind, or her emotions; she was Spirit. This short lifetime of persecution had prepared her to bring her Light into the world and to serve in a way that most are incapable of serving until their very last lifetimes.

Case AA

Monica is a very young soul who is alive today, who chose schizophrenia to increase her compassion and appreciation for the value of independence. Because Monica doesn't have Hanna's inner resources and inner strength, Monica's soul chose to be born into a supportive and understanding environment. Monica has been cared for at home under the supervision of a psychiatrist. In these modern times, Monica has had the advantages that medication can bring to this illness, allowing her to lead a relatively normal, although sheltered, existence.

It hasn't been possible for Monica to learn the same lessons as Hanna because Monica is a much younger soul. Nevertheless, Monica has learned some fundamental lessons, and this situation has also provided her with a safe environment in which to learn about a highly technological and complex world. Ordinarily, such a young soul would have reincarnated into a simpler society, where expectations of accomplishment are minimal and the basics of survival are taught patiently by family members. In Monica's case, the schizophrenic lifestyle provided this kind of support and training amidst a technological society.

You may wonder why Monica chose to be born into a technological society at all. Besides her own learning, the reason was that she had something to teach her caretakers. Her mental illness arrested her family's busy, materialistic lifestyle long enough to make them look inside themselves.

Schizophrenia, like any personal crisis, was a way of advancing the spiritual and emotional growth of Monica's family members. This illness not only demanded her parents' patience, but allowed them to appreciate the depth of love they have for their daughter and for each other. Monica's mental illness brought her family closer together and enhanced their ability to give to each other. These are not minor accomplishments but significant landmarks in the evolutionary journey.

Case BB

This story differs from the last two because the mental illness in this story was not a pre-life choice but a means for coping with an intolerable situation. When grossly abused or traumatized, younger souls often retreat from the world by becoming mentally ill. Although these individuals may not consciously choose to be mentally ill, they give up on life, and it takes this form. This choice is like suicide in its intent to escape life, but the individual remains alive while abdicating the privilege of living consciously and deliberately. Ironically, this tendency to surrender their will together with their inexperience is what makes young souls vulnerable to abuse in the first place.

Melissa was sexually abused by her father until she escaped

by leaving home. While she was on her own, she was repeatedly raped by an acquaintance. After this, she stopped participating in reality and became a ward of the state. The soul is rarely responsible for circumstances that create this much stress on someone so vulnerable. When this happens, the soul's plan has usually gone awry because of others. Although the soul will do what it can to right such a situation, sometimes it's not enough.

It might be interesting to look at how the souls of those involved tried to influence this situation. First, Melissa's soul hadn't anticipated that her father would be abusive. Since he hadn't been abusive for many lifetimes, he wasn't a likely perpetrator. When his intentions became apparent, his soul attempted to prevent the abuse by trying to influence him and others involved intuitively.

When this didn't work, Melissa's soul created an illness that required medical intervention in the hope that the physician would discover the abuse, but the physician wasn't thorough enough. Their souls even brought another woman into the picture to deflect the father's interest, but to no avail.

Sexual abuse is addictive and difficult to stop once it begins. Their souls couldn't reach Melissa's mother either because she was involved in her own addiction with alcohol. This, too, was unexpected. Melissa's mother was a sensitive woman, capable of lovingly caring for her daughter. She began drinking when she miscarried her second child. Although the miscarriage was part of the mother's soul's plan, it wasn't anticipated that she would turn this tragedy into another one by coping with it this way.

Addiction is damaging not only socially, physically, and emotionally but spiritually. It's one of the most common reasons for plans going awry, although many people turn to addictions *because* they are out of harmony with their soul's plan. Because addictions interfere with receiving the soul's messages, many who are ruled by their addictions find themselves trapped in unfulfilling lives. Even more tragic is when an addiction interferes with other people's plans, as it did in this case. Then, some future balancing might be needed, not to punish the addict but to show the addict the importance of taking charge of his or her life and not spoiling the lives of others.

Although Melissa's mental illness eventually did bring Melissa the protection she needed and some increase in compassion, it prevented her from accomplishing her other lessons. Unfortunately, when the order of one's lessons is changed, the same understandings aren't necessarily achieved. Since mental illness wasn't part of Melissa's plan, she didn't benefit from this experience as those in the previous stories had.

Since this is a present-day story, Melissa's future lifetimes are yet to be written. Melissa's future plan is likely to include a nurturing environment, one that will help her rebuild her confidence, sense of self, and trust. She's likely to choose a small town or village in which to be raised, where her safety can be better assured, and a fiery astrology chart for ego development and assertiveness. She will also need to learn to cope with the stress of life in other ways than by escaping.

Since Melissa's mother never made the connection between Melissa's mental illness and her own lack of responsibility, the mother's future healing will undoubtedly include an experience that will help her realize the damage caused by addiction. The circumstances for this lesson shouldn't be hard to arrange because she'll be predisposed to alcoholism and likely to become alcoholic again. Because addictions continue into future lifetimes, the lessons of addiction are unavoidable.

The mother's healing is also likely to entail a situation similar to her miscarriage to help her gain the spiritual understanding she missed by drowning her sorrows in alcohol. For instance, this might be accomplished by having someone close to her lose a child. With an astrology chart that fosters soul-searching (Sagittarius or Scorpio) and people who could give her the proper guidance, her chances for finding answers to the questions she formerly avoided would be good.

As for the father, a variety of issues will need to be addressed. One of them is power because incest involves an abuse of power and will. Correct use of power is usually taught by meeting the negative consequences of abusing power. Another is self-restraint, especially as it applies to thoughts, since the father's fantasies played a key role in the abuse. And the last is empathy.

Because empathy is learned by being victimized, karma that teaches empathy often looks punitive. But learning empathy is part of every soul's evolution. No one escapes this lesson, although some souls have fewer experiences of victimization than others because they learn faster. This is one instance in which the father is likely to need to be victimized in the same way his daughter was. This is how empathy is taught. His future victimization will be a consequence of—not a punishment for—abusing his daughter.

Please don't conclude from this that everyone who is abused was a perpetrator in previous lifetimes and therefore deserving of abuse, although it is true that throughout your many lifetimes, you play every role. You have made every mistake every human being has ever made, and that deserves your compassion, not your judgment or disdain.

By the way, no soul actually chooses before life to be an abuser, or a murderer for that matter. Some souls are just likely to become perpetrators out of a lack of soul development. When a soul's pre-life plan includes experiencing abuse or something similar, it chooses to be born into a family or an environment where there are likely perpetrators, young souls who lack the soul development for dealing with their emotions.

Mental Disability

Mental disability is nearly always a pre-life choice and something every soul experiences, usually in one's earlier incarnations. Intellectual limitations serve many lessons. Besides patience and compassion for those less skilled, mental disability teaches people to live moment by moment. Someone who's limited intellectually is unable to think abstractly or consider the past or future. Their world consists only of the present. In this way, they're similar to very young children or other living creatures.

Learning to be in the moment is by no means an insignificant lesson. It's central to one's later lifetimes, when the lesson is transcending the ego, or false self. The ego is the aspect of the personal self that delights in projecting itself into the future and ruminating about the past. The ego keeps people from experiencing themselves in the present, the only place where the divine self can be known. Because mental disability can bring people into the moment, old souls who want to learn to do this sometimes choose this challenge.

Case CC

This is the story of a very young soul named Jeanne who chose to experience a mild mental disability for shelter and protection from the world. Because very young souls don't have the resources or coping mechanisms for dealing with a busy world, many very young souls grow up in small villages, rural settings, institutions, or other places that provide them with the safety they need while helping them learn the basics of survival.

Jeanne was mentally disabled in a society that usually cared for such people in institutions. But Jeanne was only mildly disabled and could benefit from schooling, so she was placed in a special school and looked after by her parents. She flourished in this environment, which provided her with what she needed for her physical and emotional well-being.

Jeanne's situation was ideal, but why do many mentally disabled people find themselves in situations that aren't ideal? One answer is that sometimes the environment doesn't fulfill the soul's expectations. Because the choices of others can't be controlled, the environment doesn't always turn out as the soul intended. Another reason is that older souls might choose mental disability under difficult conditions to accelerate their growth or learn a certain lesson. Very young souls never choose a potentially abusive or neglectful situation, however, because they don't have the inner resources to benefit from it.

Those who are damaged by the experience of mental disability are usually very young souls whose environment became abusive or neglectful despite the soul's intent to the contrary. In these instances, those who've contributed to the neglect or abuse will face lessons to make sure they won't continue doing this, while the victim will need a protective environment to mend.

Because very young souls are so vulnerable, abusive situations in early lifetimes can be devastating, requiring many lifetimes of simple living and protection to heal. Needless to say, this is a real setback to the soul's progress. Many in this situation spend lifetimes in an institution or some other sheltered environment where they are cared for and their trust is rebuilt.

On the other hand, institutionalization has often been the culprit, fostering the same abuse and neglect from which some individuals are recovering. Institutions serve both those who are learning greater compassion for the neglected and abused and those recovering from neglect and abuse. Good institutions and bad ones have always existed, and the soul will use both to serve these two different purposes.

Case DD

The old soul in this story had several monastic lifetimes before a lifetime of mental disability. Because of the stifling effect of monasticism on individuality and intimate relationships, his social development and initiative were inhibited. Although his monastic lifetimes advanced him spiritually, they left other aspects of himself undeveloped. Having finally reached a point in his evolution when a devotional lifestyle was no longer beneficial, he needed other experiences to help him become more well-rounded. So, he chose to experience mental disability.

In that lifetime, he was profoundly mentally disabled and born into a large, close-knit family. This situation served several purposes. He was able to learn vicariously from this even though he was unable to process information consciously. His observations about family life and relationships were recorded by his unconscious mind and would be available to him in later lifetimes. In addition, the forced passivity aroused his desire to act on life, which balanced his former tendency to be passive. Except under such extreme circumstances, this couldn't have been achieved so quickly. And finally, it strengthened his desire to serve children and others who are helpless.

Imprisonment and Seclusion

Extensive imprisonment or seclusion invariably leaves a mark, especially if those conditions are forced and inescapable. Even when someone chooses to be cloistered away, this experience, although valuable in some respects, usually requires future balancing. One reason is that human relations, which are an integral part of life, don't exist under these conditions nor does sexuality in the fullest sense. Both imprisonment and seclusion foster habits that are usually unproductive to future relationships, as we will see in the stories that follow.

Nevertheless, imprisonment and seclusion are universal experiences from which people can benefit if they have the inner resources to grow from these experiences. Imprisonment and seclusion can increase one's appreciation for life and its small pleasures, much like poverty can. When the ego's pleasures are stripped away, as they often are in these situations, all that's left is the divine self—if you can get beyond the desires for what you don't have.

As might be expected, older souls are more capable than younger souls of using these kinds of limitations for their growth. While imprisonment can be enlightening for an old soul, it can be devastating to a very young one, so the soul avoids placing very young souls in circumstances that could lead to imprisonment. Seclusion, on the other hand, holds some potential for growth even for the youngest of souls.

Unfortunately, those who imprison others don't discriminate between young souls and old souls. Imprisonment often happens to vast numbers of people at once, most of whom do not have this as part of their soul's plan. For those whose plans are disrupted, their evolution for lifetimes to come is affected. As for those responsible for this, they'll have to realize and atone for the damage they've caused.

The following stories depict the positive and negative effects of imprisonment and seclusion. But please understand that just because imprisonment may work for good and be part of the soul's plan doesn't condone it. I'd like to underline again that it's never in someone's soul's plan to victimize someone else even if it's part of the other's plan to be victimized. Rather, the soul will put an intended victim in a situation with this potential without knowing exactly who will carry out the injustice, if anyone.

Imprisonment

Case EE

Phillip was a prisoner of war. He was tortured, maligned, and left with nothing to eat or drink. When he finally succumbed to death, he'd been left alone for over a week. This is an instance of gross injustice, regardless of what justification his oppressors might have had. If Phillip had been lacking in compassion, this experience might have resulted in bitterness and hatred lasting for lifetimes. However, Phillip was able to accept this injustice without needing to avenge it.

Hatred is undeniably the most damaging consequence of experiences like these. For a very young soul, the pain of such an experience may be translated into fear, mistrust, and hatred lasting for lifetimes. Those who've reaped hatred from such experiences will need nurturing in their next lifetimes.

Phillip didn't enter his next lifetime with hatred, but there were other negative effects. After this cruel treatment, Phillip didn't have the same trust and optimism as before. His will to live was affected too, which was important to balance. Without the will to live, people are likely to waste their life or go through it without the appreciation it deserves.

To balance this, in his next lifetime, his soul intended to show him the goodness of life. It selected a loving family and an astrology chart that would foster courage, confidence, and a zest for life (Leo). This was to be a fun and interesting lifetime, full of exploration and growth.

Unfortunately, he didn't benefit from these circumstances as he might have because he had difficulty enjoying himself when others were suffering. So, in his next lifetime (the current one), his soul shifted his energy toward service. He now works as a missionary, which gives him plenty of opportunities to express his compassion. After this lifetime, he'll probably be ready for different lessons.

This analysis wouldn't be complete without also examining what his oppressors need to balance their actions. What caused them to mistreat someone like this? The answer to this will determine what will be needed to balance these actions. Since this particular injustice was spawned by religious beliefs, the balancing would be accomplished by instilling religious tolerance. To do this, astrology charts that promote tolerance (Aquarius, Sagittarius, Gemini, and Libra) and conditions that teach this were selected.

This was accomplished for one individual by having him reincarnate into a small town where conformity was expected and religious intolerance was widespread. He was born into a family that was scorned by the community because they didn't worship like the rest of the town.

When he grew up, he was determined to find a more accepting environment, only to wind up in a similar situation elsewhere. This caused him to examine his own values and why people felt and behaved the way they did. Eventually he moved to a large city, where he met people who were more broadminded. There, he expressed his opinions about religious intolerance with the same fervor he'd expressed his religious views in his previous lifetime. At least this time, his opinions didn't hurt others or infringe on their rights.

He was unusual in how quickly he learned his lesson. Not everyone involved in the incarceration and torture learned so quickly. Another individual, a woman in her next lifetime, was born into similar circumstances but with entirely different results. She responded to the townspeople's scorn by accepting it as a just evaluation of herself and by treating others with the same disdain. She died unhappy and alone and with no more understanding than she'd come in with. It took two more lifetimes in similar circumstances before she learned to respect people's basic right to hold differing views.

The first individual suffered little in balancing the grievous acts of his former lifetime because he learned so quickly. The second individual wasn't as fortunate, taking three precious lifetimes to learn the same lesson. Both individuals were also required to make amends to the victim in addition to changing their attitudes and behavior.

Clearly, when people are receptive to learning their lessons, karma doesn't have to be so painful. Only when lessons are resisted, will more painful experiences be introduced.

Case FF

Bill was jailed for a crime he didn't commit. It was a serious crime, and he was sentenced to life in prison. Bill didn't accept incarceration. He couldn't let go of his anger and resentment. These feelings festered, absorbing energy that could have been used more productively. Because those who sentenced Bill believed they were serving justice, their future lesson, if any, might entail improving the criminal justice system.

Bill's reaction is understandable. One of the problems with the criminal justice system is that it doesn't give prisoners enough hope or incentive for change. Destroying one's hope for a better future undermines the will to live.

Under these conditions, anyone would find it difficult to

overcome despair and grow, let alone the young souls who fill most prisons. Younger souls in this position often remain angry and resentful, which is only likely to lead to more criminal behavior in the future. So, although incarceration may succeed in punishing a criminal act and in taking criminals off the streets, incarceration often does nothing to redirect or transform anger and little to prevent the act from happening again.

For his next lifetime, he needed a productive outlet for his feelings of anger and injustice. If he were to become a lawyer, he could be a watchdog for similar injustices. Arranging this wouldn't be difficult, since he would already be inclined toward this. A suitable astrology chart, the right family, and certain opportunities were arranged to attract him to that profession.

He did become a lawyer, but he quit before long because he felt overburdened by the legal profession's procedures. So, this individual's healing would have to wait for another time, which isn't unusual. Lessons are often put off and others taken up. Nevertheless, he did gain from his unjust incarceration, if only an appreciation for the plight of those unjustly accused. No one understands this like someone who's experienced it.

Case GG

Todd was also incarcerated for a crime he didn't commit, but Todd's attitude was different than Bill's. This could be attributed to his astrology chart and past-life experiences, particularly a lifetime as a judge. What he learned from that lifetime was that, regardless of its imperfections, the law serves society as best it can. This belief was deeply held and helped him accept his unjustified incarceration.

Once he accepted being incarcerated, he put his energy into making the best of it. He took advantage of the prison's meager educational opportunities and studied law. He got together with other prisoners and read through cases, examining the intricacies of each one and envisioning how they were tried. This led to many fruitful philosophical and ethical discussions.

This story turned out differently from the last one because incarceration was part of Todd's soul's plan, while incarceration wasn't part of Bill's plan. Todd's incarceration served to focus his energies on the law, a former topic of interest, and uplift others. Any challenge that is part of the soul's plan will be easier to handle than a challenge that's outside it. If the challenge is part of the soul's plan, an astrology chart and an early environment will have been chosen to help the person grow and learn from that challenge. If not, the astrology chart, environment, and past-life experiences may even work against growing from that challenge.

Seclusion

Case HH

Tuku grew up in a remote part of the world with just a small tribe to call his family. Although he wasn't unhappy, he was intent on living apart from even this small band of people. There comes a time in everyone's evolution when the life of a hermit is appropriate and beneficial. For Tuku, the choice to live apart was clear and right.

Seclusion can be beneficial because it teaches self-sufficiency, responsibility, practicality, and independence. In being secluded from others and from society, people meet the consequences of their choices directly, with no one else to lean on or blame. This kind of lifestyle is particularly helpful for fairly young souls because it forces them to rely on themselves and develop their survival skills.

If someone would benefit from seclusion, but he or she is too complacent to choose it, the soul might arrange it. Younger souls are especially apt to become complacent, accepting the help of others even when they can provide for themselves and others. When this happens, the soul might arrange a shipwreck, a natural disaster, a war, or other circumstance to force the individual to become more independent.

Tuku took easily to seclusion since he had experience with it. In his previous lifetime, he'd been forced to care for himself when his parents died and left him to tend to their land and livestock. During that lifetime, he didn't have an opportunity to socialize or marry. This balanced a former pattern of dependency that had become unhealthy.

After several lifetimes of dependency and then seclusion, Tuku lacked social skills, and his next lifetimes would have to focus on developing those skills. The danger of not following lifetimes of seclusion with lifetimes of relationship is that one may lose interest in relationships altogether. Relationship may come to feel too foreign and demanding, making avoidance more attractive than engagement. Once this pattern is established, it can be difficult to break.

Case II

This is the story of someone who continued to lead fairly secluded lifetimes despite his soul's efforts to the contrary. Even lifetimes as a woman didn't dissuade him from avoiding companionship. Apparently, his lifetimes of solitude were rewarding, and he saw no reason to live with others. Only after many lifetimes alone did he finally have an experience that proved to him the importance of relationship.

One day, he found himself trapped in a snowdrift, unable to

move. Someone with a dog, who was searching for people who might have been trapped by the storm, found him. Because he needed several weeks of care, a neighbor came by regularly to attend to him. He was so touched by her kindness that he vowed to do the same for someone else sometime. It wasn't enough anymore just to take care of himself. His soul had finally gotten through to him, and the energy of his astrology chart, which fostered service and relationship, was activated.

He had two more lifetimes of service with some involvement in relationships, but his relationships lacked intimacy. He cared for others but didn't allow them to care for him. By shunning dependence, he closed the door to greater intimacy. Despite his soul's efforts to create experiences of intimacy, he remained aloof from his partners.

Even though he didn't master the lessons of intimacy, he gained enough understanding about relationships from these lifetimes to be allowed to choose another lifetime apart from intimate relationships. This time, he chose to be a priest, where he could serve without being intimate. As long as he can continue to grow through such choices without inhibiting his progress in other ways, he'll probably be allowed to. But sometime he'll have to face the lessons of intimacy again and master them, since they are part of everyone's evolution.

Conclusion

We have seen that all of your experiences—or lack of them—color your psychology and behavior. You are unique composites of everything you've ever experienced. All your previous experiences and all the astrology charts you've ever had influence your psychology in a given lifetime. This is obvious with twins, who have nearly identical charts but different ways of responding to the energies of those charts. Even identical twins aren't clones of each other. This is because they bring to the expression of their charts everything they've learned in former lifetimes. Once this is understood, the personality can be appreciated for what it is: a vehicle for the soul's evolution.

The task of evolution is not to do away with the personality. That would be impossible and undesirable. Evolution uses the personality to learn the lessons of this reality. But in your later lifetimes, a different relationship to your personality is established: The divine self begins to express itself increasingly through the personality instead of the ego.

This shift doesn't come about through your own efforts or will but naturally and gradually in the course of your evolution. Meditation and awareness can hasten this natural process. The kingdom of God is not won by force but by mastering the personality's lessons. You evolve by learning to express your personality positively.

Since your personality is the vehicle for your soul's evolution, it's important to understand it and use it for your growth. Once you have a sense of your personality and its traits, as described in your astrology chart, then ask yourself why these traits are part of your life now. A trait is part of your personality for one of four reasons:

1. You chose that trait to help you accomplish your life purpose. For example, Aries, which confers independence and courage, might be chosen if your life purpose requires leadership.

2. You chose that trait to balance a destructive pattern established in a former lifetime, possibly due to a trauma. For example, Leo gives courage, which could neutralize a fear of something.

3. That trait was developed and ingrained through repetition in past lives. For example, you might be very meticulous even without any Virgo in your astrology chart because meticulousness (a Virgo trait) was practiced or required in many of your lifetimes.

4. You are learning the lessons that accompany that trait. The twelve signs represent the lessons necessary to the soul's evolution. When the time comes for a certain lesson, you're born under the appropriate sign. For example, if you're born under Aries, you are learning self-direction and independence and the lessons that come with that, such as correct use of your energy and will.

There comes a time late in your evolution when you've mastered your basic lessons and balanced most of your karma, and all that remains are minor refinements of your lessons. Then, it's time to contribute your wisdom and talents to humanity in some form of service.

How you choose to serve depends on your past experiences and the preferences and talents you've developed. Some serve by inventing or discovering things, while others serve by producing beautiful works of art or happy children. Everyone has something to offer when the time comes. But just as you need to learn the lessons of childhood before you can function as an adult, you need to master the basic human lessons before you can contribute to the world as fully as possible.

You're here not only to learn your lessons and develop your talents, but to help others do the same. Whether you realize it or not, the universe uses you to bring about other people's lessons. Each of you is deeply interconnected and intimately valuable to each other's soul's plans. Everyone's lessons touch the lives of many, each in a different way. Greta, who was stirred into service by the plight of her paralyzed friend, was touched as much by the lesson of being paralyzed as her friend was.

This is why it's so important not to interfere with someone else's soul's plan. Doing so disrupts the entire web of lessons connected to that person. You can't affect or remove anyone from the web of life without it affecting many others. Yet human beings have the power to do this.

How different the world would be if people didn't interfere with the soul's plans of others! Life is made more difficult and tragic by having the freedom to harm others; and yet, free will is necessary for evolution. If only everyone knew how to use their will better.

It's easy to blame God for the injustices in life—poverty, disease, and death—without fully appreciating the role that your choices play. Much of the sorrow in the world wouldn't exist if everyone made sounder, more compassionate choices. What is termed evil is often the result of uninformed and unenlightened choices. As long as some people on this planet are still learning the basic lessons of life, there will be evil acts. As older souls, you have a duty to help these less informed and less enlightened souls learn, heal, and grow.

One opportunity for helping younger souls grow is through reforming the criminal justice system, which is failing miserably. Just as religions need to shift their focus from retribution, so do prisons. Before this can be done, people will have to agree that human beings are innately good. If some are believed to be evil, they'll be treated inhumanely and they won't heal. No one is born evil, but many are born with a great deal of fear and a lack of wisdom, which can result in evil acts, especially when compounded by abuse or neglect.

This problem isn't solved by imprisoning people, where many are further abused. Imprisonment might serve many valid purposes, but healing isn't one of them. Criminals are as much in need of healing as their victims. Unless their healing is addressed, hatred and violence will continue.

The tragedy of the criminal justice system is that this population, which is so much in need of healing, doesn't receive it. You've seen how the soul heals people by providing a nurturing environment and role models and opportunities to develop some talent or skill to build self-esteem. You know these ingredients are healing—you apply them in healing the victims. Why is it so hard to see that criminals need the same help as part of their rehabilitation?

Fear of your own dark side causes you to treat criminals as if they were subhuman or as if their ignorance and imperfections were contagious. Fear is at the root of your treatment of criminals, just as it is at the root of their treatment of others.

This fear prevents people from feeling the compassion that all human beings deserve. How can people claim to be worthy of being their wardens when they can't do it compassionately? Those who harm others might not deserve freedom, but they do deserve compassion and help. As it is, the treatment of criminals heaps more injury on them, only delaying the healing that could be begun.

The Law of Karma doesn't punish; it heals and teaches. The hope in presenting these stories is that they will inspire people to work toward improving the world by teaching and caring for others. Many people in this world need healing. Even if healing can't be completed in this lifetime, it can at least be begun. No love is ever lost on someone regardless of how it may seem. You must believe this and carry on humanely and compassionately toward everyone. You must treat everyone as you would like to be treated.

The seed of your divinity is within you even in your earliest incarnations. You are never really separate from the Divine. Your souls are always present, trying to guide you throughout your evolution. But in your earliest lifetimes, you function primarily from your ego and have more difficulty responding to your soul's guidance. This is why younger souls need the help of older, wiser souls. It is your responsibility to do what you can to help all people. Ultimately, any improvement you make in the lives of others will also improve your own.

Fortunately, your lifetimes on the physical plane eventually lead to greater love and compassion. This compassion is often taught through the experience of victimization. At some time, everyone has been a victim and everyone has been a perpetrator. These two roles are two sides of the same coin, which teaches compassion. This compassion underlies the service that is the hallmark of your later incarnations.

If your physical incarnations were all there is, then the suffering that human beings experience might be difficult to justify, just as suffering is difficult to understand within the context of just one life. But in light of your entire existence, this suffering is a small price to pay for the wisdom and understanding you gain.

The physical plane is a school, preparing you for an eternity of growth and service in nonphysical realms. The wisdom, love, and understanding you gain from your physical incarnations will be used to serve the Divine and all of creation. Your service, then, will be not only to physical systems like your own, but to nonphysical systems of reality.

Within the Great Plan, each of you is uniquely important and equally significant. Furthermore, you are mutually dependent on and irredeemably intertwined with each other. Ignorance of this truth doesn't diminish it. The recognition of this comes by opening your hearts to the possibility that within everyone lies a spark of divinity that unites all human beings. Once you become open to this truth, you can't help but discover it.

Despite how it may seem, you are not long on this earth. Your physical incarnations are infinitesimally brief within the scheme of your existence. But within the Great Plan, these lifetimes are infinitely precious, laying the foundation for all that lies ahead. You are blessed with the gift of life, but you have to make it what it can be. You may have no choice about existing or evolving, but you have every choice in *how* you will do this. Please carry on with faith in your purpose and determination to act in the highest good of all.

CHAPTER 5

Death and Dying

How to Prepare for Your Death Throughout Life

The things you do on the spiritual path—the teachings you integrate and the practices you perform—prepare you for meeting your death, as do your challenges. In life, death is another challenging event, perhaps the most challenging one. So, it stands to reason that the strengths you developed as a result of your challenges are ones you'll need and use as you face your death or what might be your death. You'll need courage and fortitude as well as patience, surrender, acceptance, compassion, and love—all developed along the way as you face life's difficulties.

In addition to these qualities, being able to be present is your most important asset as you face death. Being present is learning to be present to life as it is despite any thoughts about yourself and your life. Being present is learning to just be here in the present moment without thoughts of any kind and experiencing life as it is, without the ego's spin and stories about life. These stories, or opinions, preferences, judgments, comparisons, desires, imaginations, and fantasies, which you often give voice to, are all the ego really is—just the thoughts that continually arise in your mind, which seem important and true and like your own thoughts. This is the ego that is vanquished on the spiritual path and through meditation—just thoughts.

The reason being present is so important in times of challenge is that the qualities of your true nature, such as courage and acceptance, and the wisdom you need in a critical time are available only when you're not involved in your thoughts, which pretend to have answers to your dilemmas and crises but do not. The voice in your head will provide instructions for how to behave in any circumstance if you let it, but those instructions don't come from wisdom but from programmed information.

This information has some value, but it isn't suited to a particular moment, and that's the problem. What you've learned throughout your life, including any beneficial conditioning, is only so helpful in difficult situations. Something else is needed: wisdom. Wisdom is knowing how and when to apply that information and more. The "more" are things you do not and cannot know about a situation but which those guiding you on other dimensions do know and use to assist you.

In all your endeavors, you are helped to respond to life in the most beneficial way. In every moment, you're given helpful instructions through your intuition. These instructions come from guides and other higher dimensional beings who have your best interests at heart and who know much more than you do about how to handle a situation. If you let them, they'll guide your hand, so to speak, so that you make decisions in the moment that will be in the highest good of everyone involved.

You are always being given this guidance, but only some of you are aware of it. You will only be aware of it if you aren't actively thinking about something, since thinking blocks the flow of intuition. If you're paying attention to your thoughts, you won't notice what's in your environment—what reality is presenting you with. And you won't notice the subtle insights, urges, nudges, and other information that are being supplied to you from higher dimensions to handle the situation.

Always, there are two ways of responding to life: on the basis of your false self's advice and perspective, supplied by the voice in your head, or on the basis of your true self's perceptions, which include what's happening in the here and now and guidance from higher dimensions about how to best handle that.

In critical situations, guidance from above often breaks through even for those who are generally not tuned in to it. Even those who are very ego involved and believe nothing metaphysical can have a firsthand experience of supernatural intervention in such times, such as a voice telling them: "Stop!" or an unseen hand pushing them out of danger. Nonbelievers do sometimes become believers in times of crisis or near-death, as angels and other guides make themselves known if they deem that necessary.

Those who are nearing death will soon discover what lies beyond the death of the body, so knowledge of the other side at the time of death is often allowed to bleed into this life if it will be helpful, and it often is. Such experiences are often part of the dying process. Crisis and death are times when this is allowed, for too much bleed-through of the other realms would be confusing and distracting in everyday life. As you approach death, it's so important that you understand that a beautiful life beyond death exists. But it's less helpful to know this while you're in the midst of living your life, as this may cause you to long to be somewhere other than in the life your soul has chosen.

Near-death experiences, where someone gets a direct glimpse into life after death and then returns to life to tell about it are also evidence of what lies beyond death, and these experiences serve the person and those around that person when they do happen. But if this happened too commonly, it might be difficult for people to be fully engaged in the life their soul has chosen for them. You need to be absorbed in life and in fully being the character you've come to play in order to learn what you came to learn and do what you came to do. There's plenty of time after life, in between lifetimes, to discover that you are much more than that character. But for the time being, there is value in believing that you are this limited character.

Death is a time to fully imbibe the sweetness of having been this character. Like watching the final act in a movie about a character you loved, at death, one often perceives this character from the soul's point of view and realizes how very precious that life has been and how very sweet life is. This is seen clearly by those dying who are able to be present in the final days or weeks or months of their life. It is the potential gift of a terminal illness, where one often has time to recognize how very precious life is. This sweetness is the reward for being able to be present while dying.

Being present is a state of consciousness that is achieved by no longer indulging in thoughts about the past or the future or even about the present. It is a state of not thinking or of ignoring thoughts, which isn't easy to achieve without a dedicated practice of meditation. So, as I have so often said, meditation is the most important thing you can do for a happy life and, I will add, for a happy death.

You may think that it serves to survey your life at the end: what was good and what was not so good, what you did right and where you were mistaken. This kind of rumination about the past is generally considered normal and even healthy as one approaches death. However, I will argue that it's just such rumination that makes for an unhappy end of life, for what is it that is thinking and evaluating your life? It's the ego, of course, and it will surely make you wrong right up to the very end of your life if you let it. This is the opposite of what happens at the life review once you've left your body, in the company of your guides and others who love you. They are able to give you a loving and wise perspective on your life, which the ego is incapable of doing.

Please don't fall prey to believing that thinking about your life and evaluating it at the end of your life is necessary or desirable at death—or even in the midst of your life. It is not. Your mind will only compare yourself with others and imagine "what ifs" and find fault with life, all of which is useless and essentially untrue. That which thinks and evaluates isn't wise and is incapable of seeing you as you truly are. This aspect of yourself will only leave you feeling bad or bitter. Thinking about your life or your death is no way to prepare for your death. The mind is not capable of preparing you for death. It is what must be dispensed with at the end of life.

And, of course, thinking about a future that will never be (and which never has been real) will not serve you either at the end of your life. People often imagine all they'll miss—the weddings and births of their offspring for generations, for example. What would be the point of this? This is just what the ego does, of course. It thinks about an imaginary future that it will never experience, which evokes sad feelings. Such feelings are so unnecessary. Why make yourself sad over an imagination, something unreal? This has always been *the* recipe for suffering: wishing life were different than it is.

The best way to prepare for your death is to learn to be in each new moment fully and with a positive outlook, without living in a fantasy of some future. In other words, say yes to what life is presenting you with right now—love it, or at least accept it—and let that be enough. Stay in the here and now and enjoy that, for that's all you really have.

All those wonderful feelings you may drum up by imagining some lovely future will only cause you to miss the beauty of this moment. Fantasies make you disappointed with life, which doesn't match anyone's fantasies because fantasies don't include the challenges and other difficulties of life. You must learn to love life as it is, difficulties and all, and fantasies won't help you with that. They only make you discontent with yourself and with life. Learn to love life as it is, and you'll be happy, and you'll be happy at the end of your life as well.

Life is loveable just as it, and comparing it to some fantasy is how you take yourself out of the life you are given and make yourself unhappy. *You* make yourself unhappy, nothing else. Learn to be happy now with now, and you'll be happy even at death. This is what I most want you to understand. You can be happy regardless of what you're experiencing if you learn to love whatever you're experiencing. Love the gift that life is, no matter what is happening. That's what life is all about—learning to love it all. By love, I simply mean saying, "Yes, this too is life" rather than "No, I don't want to experience this." It's in saying "No!" that you create your suffering. Say "Yes!" instead, and you cannot suffer even at death.

Is Every Death God's Will?

Not every death happens because it's your time to go. It may not be God's will that you die at a particular time in a particular way, but it is God's will that you learn from your mistakes, and if you cause your own death, you may need to learn from that. Many deaths are self-created and allowed by God, if you will, or the soul, because they serve the soul's growth. They teach a particular lesson. Nevertheless, it might not have been the soul's intention that you die just then and in that way, but the soul can gain from any experience. On the other hand, you all know of instances of people escaping death quite miraculously, and in those cases, it is quite easy to conclude that it was not that person's time to go.

As you can imagine, the lessons related to one's death in a particular manner at a particular time are too numerous to name and can't really be known. Why do people die when they do? Death may be the result of some choice they made, or their death may have been designed by their soul to serve some purpose, either in their individual growth or for the collective. Or, in relatively rare instances, death may be the result of an accident, an event that was unintended and perhaps not foreseen by the soul.

Sometimes the soul isn't able to prevent an accident that results in death or bodily harm. This is relatively rare because, in most cases, angelic intervention is possible, and many have experienced just this. If it isn't someone's time to go and there is good reason to continue one's life and not a good reason to leave at that point, higher dimensional beings will intervene to save a person's life or save them from harm. How successfully they're able to do that depends on the situation.

In everyone's life, there are several points at which the soul might choose to leave the body. When that is depends on a number of things, which can't be determined before life because the life story is not predetermined and written before life. It's played out as you go along, depending on your choices and the choices of others. The soul will choose to leave at a time when it can benefit from that death in some way. The soul rarely wastes an opportunity to learn from a death, and in any event, it is impossible not to learn something from such an event.

I would be remiss if I didn't add that sometimes people don't learn a lesson sufficiently the first time, and then they're bound to encounter similar circumstances in other lifetimes until they do. Those who are foolhardy, for instance, might die several deaths while pushing their limits before they change course and are done with that lesson or have exhausted all the various lessons related to pushing one's limits.

The soul doesn't shy away from experiencing any kind of death or death at a young age, for instance, if that serves its purpose. The soul is in the business of growing and learning, and it is willing to have any experience.

What the Soul Gains from Death

Each death in your various lifetimes brings so much growth for your soul. There are so many ways that you die in your many lifetimes, and every way teaches something different. Life is full of lessons, and some of the most powerful and important lessons are learned in your last moments of life or in the months leading up to one's death, in the case of a terminal illness.

Life often feels unfair, and painful and difficult deaths often feel unfair, but they are always wise from the standpoint of your soul. Your soul chooses the type of death you will have because it serves your soul's growth to have that experience. You are never being punished. Every death you have undergone has always been chosen or allowed by your soul because that experience was deemed to have something to offer you in terms of your growth.

Whether you do grow from that experience and how much is up to you to some extent, but even the most resistant and angry person is learning something that will change how he or she is in subsequent lifetimes. As I've said many times, you can't help but learn from your various experiences, even if it appears to you or to others that you aren't learning or haven't learned anything.

One's apparent reactions to an experience such as death, such as anger, sadness, bitterness, and resistance, are the ego's response to a situation and don't accurately reflect the deeper effect of that experience. You learn in spite of any anger, sadness, bitterness, or resistance. While these emotions are happening on the surface, deep changes on other levels are going on that are often imperceptible to the one dying and those witnessing the death. After death, when the individual looks back on that experience in the life review, the lesson becomes obvious, and the individual can feel gratitude for even that experience.

There is great wisdom in the design of one's life and experiences. Learning is built into life in ways you can't imagine. For instance, when something horrific happens, such as child abuse, this can serve the soul by developing the person's compassion or driving that person into a healing profession or one supportive of children, such as education or child welfare. Many life purposes are founded on just such intense experiences that drive one's interest in a particular direction, often for many consecutive lifetimes. Souls gain in wisdom and skill and become specialists in an area by taking on similar life purposes over a series of lifetimes.

A difficult death also often drives a soul to pursue a particular life purpose in subsequent lifetimes. For instance, someone might become a doctor or nurse in the next lifetime because he or she was inspired to serve in that way by a difficult death. Or perhaps someone who was fatally shot will become an advocate for gun control or peace in the next lifetime.

And, of course, difficult deaths also balance certain weaknesses and cultivate strengths. For example, someone who died as a result of a reckless or foolhardy act will be much more cautious in the next lifetime. Or someone who murdered someone might lose someone dear in his or her next lifetime. Please understand, however, that such losses are never punishment but intended to help people gain empathy and learn the preciousness of life. And please don't conclude that every loss in your life is such a teaching. There are many reasons for losses, not the least of which is that loss is a natural part of life.

But most of all, the lessons at death are spiritual ones: As people grapple with the loss of the things that give them identity, they discover who they really are and what can never be lost. Who are you if you are no longer young and capable? Who are you when your body stops working? What is it that exists beyond the body? Are you still you? What are you still capable of?

What many discover as their body ages or becomes incapacitated is that their body and looks actually have little to do with who they are. They're still the same inside, the same consciousness, and they still have the same personality and tendencies. These are the things that make them who they are and make them unique.

For those who are overly identified with their looks and physicality, aging and becoming incapacitated offer particularly important lessons, but everyone is deeply identified with the physical body and needs to see that the body is not that important in terms of who they are. They have a body, but they are not the body. They are the consciousness that uses the body. They are what exists beyond the body.

Importantly, they are what loves and laughs and experiences life. Sometimes this is all one is able to do, and then you can discover that loving, laughing, and experiencing is enough—enough to make you happy. This is one of the most advanced lessons that can be learned. When everything is stripped away, there's still the ability to love and to experience and, potentially, to laugh and be grateful for life. What a surprise!

Most people think they need so much to be happy, and to discover that, indeed, so little is actually needed is the most wonderful discovery of all! How freeing it is to find happiness in simply existing and in loving whatever you're loving, which could be anything. Everything is worthy of love.

Life becomes very precious for many at the end of their lives. They see life in a way that they've never seen it before. They see through their divine self's eyes, and it is all good and all precious. Granted, this doesn't happen for everyone, but the potential exists to experience this if you don't get overly caught up in anger, frustration, regret, and other negativity, as you continue to think of yourself as the false self and continue to want the same things the false self always wants.

It's impossible to be happy at the end of life if you continue to want the things your ego or false self wants. That's why death is such a powerful spiritual catalyst. To not suffer greatly at death, you must, once and for all, give up the desires and dreams of the false self. When you do, you discover the grace, love, peace, and gratitude of the divine self.

This is the blessing of a terminal illness. The knowledge that death is imminent takes away your future. When you believe you no longer have a future, what good are your desires and dreams? All you have is now. A terminal illness teaches you to be in the Now like nothing else because it strips away your future, and with your future, go your dreams and desires for your life to be a certain way.

Nevertheless, many hang onto life while they are terminally ill, still hoping for a future rather than accepting the life they are having and delving into that experience—the rich experience of their body and their identities falling away, which is a most precious and profound experience.

For some, giving up the false self's desires and dreams will be impossible. However, that doesn't mean they failed at death or that they didn't learn something, for they have another chance to see things differently once they're out of the body and shown by guides and loved ones how life and death might have been different.

In the afterlife, you're able to look back on your life without feeling bad or regretful that your life or death didn't go better. It becomes obvious that nothing is lost. No harm has been done. The divine spark of God is there, alive and well, as you exist in the afterlife.

In the afterlife, you're able to experience your divinity in a way that you might not have been able to when you were alive. In the afterlife, you're in touch with the truth about yourself, so viewing your previous lifetime's flaws and mistakes is not painful but enlightening. Like watching a movie of someone who didn't know any better, you're steeped in the forgiveness and compassion of those who are helping you see the truth about your life, so the life review is actually quite joyous.

It's impossible to list all of the possible things you do learn from the various kinds of deaths, but I will do my best to try to give you a sense of this. In addition to learning that you are not the body, which terminal illness teaches masterfully, death also teaches many of the basic lessons that human beings must master.

Importantly, death teaches compassion and empathy as a result of the suffering that's often involved in both the death itself and the anticipation of death. Whenever there's great suffering, compassion is being learned, whether that's apparent or not. Experiencing difficulties gives you compassion for those undergoing those same difficulties. You've walked in their shoes, and you know what it's like.

The various deaths are some of the most important and intense experiences your soul will ever have, and it's important that everyone have these experiences, because they are rich with rewards. As with all the extreme challenges of life, your many deaths teach you things you can't learn any other way. They develop character, which is to say, they develop you spiritually.

What do I mean by this? For one thing, death is humbling, and humility is central to one's spiritual growth. What is humbled? The ego, of course. Its greatest desire is to be in control of life. This is also its greatest illusion, for it has little control over what happens in life. At death, it becomes inescapably clear that you are not in control of life. As people face the fact that their life—their story—is about to end, they often feel regretful: "Is that it?" They want the story to continue or to be able to rewrite it, but they never *were* able to make life be the way they wanted it to be and neither can they at death. This is humbling, and this must be accepted.

Even those who have had what would be considered very successful lives are often disappointed at the end of their life, since the ego can always think of something more it would like to do or have or have experienced. For the ego, life as it is, is never enough. This disappointment in the face of death is, unfortunately, very common. But if it can be seen that this disappointment is just the ego's constant state and not a measure of one's life, then acceptance of life as it is and death is possible.

At death, you face what your life is and what your life was. The story has an ending after all. It is what it is, and it was what it was, and this must be accepted. Acceptance is one of the greatest lessons in life, and it isn't mastered until your very last lifetimes.

Death helps you see that you are not the master of the universe or immortal. You are flesh and bones like everyone else. Any grandiose illusions your ego might have had must be placed at the feet of death. It is an unavoidable ending to everyone's story, but not an ending to you, surprisingly enough, as you soon find out.

Death, especially one preceded by illness, is often an exercise in forbearance, patience, acceptance, and living in the unknown, as you wait and wonder at each step: "What will be the outcome?" You have always lived in the unknown (you have never known what would happen), but in critical times, you wonder, "Is this it? Will this end in death? Is this how I die?" You don't know, and you must accept that you don't know.

You'll never know the answer to the question, "When will I die?" until you actually do. Living in the unknown can be especially challenging when you're ill: "Will I recover? What if...? What will happen next?" These are questions the ego desperately wants answered but ones it can never have answers for. With illness and death, the ego has met its match. It's stymied, frustrated, unable to continue as usual. With grave illness or with terminal illness, the ego faces the greatest challenge of all, one it will eventually lose.

What, hopefully, rises up in place of the ego is the strength, courage, peace, perseverance, patience, and compassion of the divine self. Grave illness and death are opportunities for these qualities to come to the surface, for the divine self to shine through and become known and expressed.

What is left when the body can no longer function? All of the qualities that make up the best of you: courage, kindness, patience, strength, wisdom, love, and perseverance. If you are so lucky as to have the ego drop away during an illness or before death, you are left with who you really are, and that is magnificent!

What Happens Just Before Death

One's death and transition to the afterlife are eased enormously when someone has time to prepare psychologically and spiritually for his or her death. This is one of the benefits of a terminal illness. Not only is there time to connect with loved ones, put affairs in order, and prepare mentally by reading spiritual teachings and getting advice from those who understand this process, but other dimensional forces have time to prepare the person for this remarkable experience.

The most important preparations for transition to the afterlife are accomplished through interactions with other dimensions. As death approaches, the dying spend increasingly more time in other dimensions, while asleep and otherwise, where they receive comfort, healing, and instruction about death and what they need to understand about the life they are leaving.

As the person begins to lose his or her grip on life, a kind of life review begins, when possible. At a certain point in the dying process, most become receptive to reviewing their life from a higher perspective. This life review takes place during visitations from higher dimensional beings, including angels, who help the individual forgive and let go of the past, since hanging on in these ways can interfere with a peaceful transition. This forgiveness process is a prelude to the much more extensive life review individuals will have once they've crossed over.

While in sleep or in an in-between state, which the dying spend much of their time in, higher dimensional beings assist them in accepting their death and do what they can to help them welcome it. They explain to them what they'll experience and arrange for loved ones who've crossed over to visit them in their dreams and while awake. It's not uncommon for those nearing death to have visions of these angels, guides, and departed loved ones and to hear voices. These visions may be experienced with their eyes open or closed.

Often their departed loved ones have a message to deliver that's meaningful to them. But just their joyful and loving presence is enough to help the one dying relax and begin to look forward to seeing them again in the afterlife, for most who are dying believe that will be the case once they die. This belief is confirmed by these visitations from departed loved ones, who tell them they'll be seeing them soon in a place of great beauty and freedom, including freedom from pain and the current limitations of their body.

Messages of comfort and love are also delivered to the dying by the angels, guides, and other light beings in attendance, who may take the form of religious figures, such as myself, or I may actually be present when there's an especially strong connection with me. All this helps give the one dying a sense of a new life, making it easier to leave the old one behind. As a result, many who are at the end of life embrace death when it does finally arrive.

Those who die suddenly don't have these advantages that would help them adjust to their new state of being. Sudden death can be overwhelmingly shocking and likely to require help from guides and departed loved ones who are skillful at dealing with such events. A period of healing nearly always accompanies death for all but very old souls, and this is all the more necessary in the event of sudden death or suicide.

What Happens After Death

Many people struggle with being afraid of dying, mostly because of what they believe about death and dying. I would like to say some, hopefully, comforting things about death to ease your minds and hearts about this great mystery.

Death is not the end of your existence—not by far! You are eternal beings. What I mean by this is that your soul was spun off of All That Is, the Oneness, and will eventually return or remerge with the Oneness, or Source, but even that is not a death but a reunion of the most glorious kind, for when you exist as All That Is, you know nothing but love and joy—eternally. So, although your individual soul is not eternal, the consciousness that takes on a soul and evolves through the physical plane and other nonphysical dimensions is eternal. You *are* God. Literally.

This is difficult to take in and understand while you are in a human body. Your humanness is so convincing! Even once you're awakened or become enlightened, you still experience yourself as human, and that will continue to be so for most even after they leave their body. Most retain their sense of being human in between lifetimes as long as they are still reincarnating. After death, some personality and certain tendencies and interests remain while you exist on the astral plane. How much you retain this sense of being human depends on your level of evolution and other things.

Since it's difficult for you to realize that you are divine, you'll have to take my word for this: You are not human. You are essentially divine, meaning you are made of the stuff that God is made of, and for lack of a better word, this "stuff" is called consciousness or love.

Both of these words point to something intangible, mysterious, and difficult to say much else about. Words fail in describing your essential nature, since words weren't designed for such things. Words were designed to describe *things,* and you are not a thing, although you may feel like you are your particular body-mind. However, that is simply the conception of the mind, the best the mind can do to comprehend the mystery of who you are. The closest *thing* to what you are would naturally be thought to be your body-mind, so your mind conceives of you as your body-mind.

It's actually quite obvious to something other than the mind—to consciousness, to who you really are—that you are much different than your body-mind. Who you really are knows who you really are! And from *this* standpoint, it isn't hard to see that the body-mind is simply an instrument for the consciousness that enlivens the body-mind.

And so, we can speak about your essence as what enlivens the body-mind, for the body-mind is nothing lasting and quickly disintegrates without this mysterious life force or consciousness. When you see a body that is no longer enlivened by this force, it's obvious that that body is no longer inhabited by what made that person uniquely himself or herself and that it no longer contains the essence of that person. The light has gone out; the consciousness has left, and it is just flesh and bones, discarded by the soul so that it can continue its journey in another form, a nonphysical one for the time being.

So, where does the soul go after death, in between lifetimes? This is one of the most common questions, and I'll try to answer this as simply as I can, although the answer is not so simple. Different souls go to different places within the astral plane, which is the nonphysical dimension just a little higher than yours in vibration. The quote from the Bible, "My Father's house has many mansions" refers to the many different places within the astral plane and also the many dimensions beyond the astral plane. What determines where you go on the astral plane after death is your level of consciousness and what your previous human selves want to experience and explore and also what your soul needs in order to grow and heal.

No matter where you land on the astral plane, a great deal of healing and growth is bound to occur, since that's the purpose for being on the astral plane in between lives. Just as the earthly plane is about growth and about healing the misconceptions and misperceptions of the human journey so that you can rediscover the love at your core, the astral plane is also about healing any misconceptions and misperceptions you still carry as a human being.

This is good news—that so much growth and healing occur in between lives. It may seem like many die without having learned much. However, from your vantage point, it's impossible to evaluate how much a soul has learned or will learn from a particular lifetime. It may seem like someone has learned nothing or even regressed and devolved, but that's never the case.

The beings guiding your soul will help you learn from the lifetime you've just left through a detailed and compelling life review. In this life review, you not only see how you were affected by others, but how you affected others. You get to see "behind the scenes" in a way that was impossible when you were alive. You finally get to know some of the things you couldn't have known while you were alive. Just as you observe a movie character and understand things about that character that the character doesn't see about himself or herself and know what the other characters think about that character, you come to see yourself, others, and your life choices more objectively.

At last, you're given the clarity and higher perspective you need to love yourself, love others, and love life, and you feel the deepest compassion for yourself and those you've been involved with. You see where you haven't measured up, and you're shown how you might have behaved differently and had a different outcome.

Through the life review, your guides attempt to motivate you to correct your failings and do things differently so that you'll experience less suffering and more love next time around. The role you played in your own suffering and the suffering you caused others becomes clear to you, and the pain of that usually motivates one to do things differently next time. The life review changes people, and this review is often where the most growth is accomplished.

There's a catch, however: Although you see your life, your mistakes, and your weaknesses very clearly as a result of this review, once you reincarnate, your previous conditioning and misunderstandings will still prevail to some extent, at least initially. You'll still behave in many of the ways you used to in your previous lifetime or lifetimes, but your failings will be much easier to see through and overcome as a result of the coaching you received on the other side. You'll have some access to the wisdom you gained when you were between lifetimes. The life review is, to a great extent, where wisdom comes from.

The more lifetimes you've lived, the more practice you've had at overcoming the issues entailed in being human—the arrogance, fear, selfishness, impatience, carelessness, irresponsibility, judgment, and so on that cause you to be unkind and make poor choices. As you evolve through your many lifetimes, you become a wiser and more loving person, and you naturally make better choices. Older souls have a much easier time on the physical plane than younger souls because of all they've learned throughout their many lifetimes. This learning is stored in their soul, and they have access to it through their intuition.

This explains why some people are more naturally and more easily loving and wise, while others struggle so much. There is really no other way to learn what you need to learn as a human being than by making mistake after mistake and learning from those mistakes. The soul is not the least bit impatient with this process, but of course the ego is, and patience with this process is also one of the lessons.

I said that there are many "mansions," or places, on the astral plane that people go after they die. After death, nearly everyone experiences a period of healing, since death is often traumatic for a person, even if there was no actual trauma. So many have false ideas about death that cause them to suffer unnecessarily, and those false ideas need to be healed, or seen as false. So, the first step for most souls is healing of some sort.

One of the problems with some religious ideas is the fear they induce about what comes after death. Christianity, for one, in its belief in hell and punishment after death, causes so much unnecessary pain and fear for people before dying and even after dying. When people are full of self-hatred, regret, or deeply depressed, they are taken to an astral hospital of sorts to help them heal those emotions and see life more clearly and truly.

This healing is not so easy to accomplish when guilt and fear are deeply inculcated by religion or otherwise because it's often difficult to convince such people who've crossed over that they have nothing to fear and that they won't be experiencing punishment. Religious beliefs about hell keep many in a hell of sorts of their own making. Because they believe in hell, they insist on experiencing it, and so some do suffer for a while before they're willing to accept the truth—that they are loved and forgiven and allowed to have a good and happy life on the astral plane.

And then, there are those who remain attached to earth because they have addictions, fears, or trauma that prevent them from moving on from that lifetime. When one's body has been physically addicted to alcohol or drugs, for instance, the individual is often drawn to continuing to experience that addiction through those who are still alive by attaching to their energy field and possibly influencing them through the voice in their head. Such disembodied humans hang around drug addicts or people in bars and encourage their addiction because they're able to live vicariously to some extent through such people.

Some disembodied souls are also very afraid of experiencing and exploring their new home on the astral or they believe they're unworthy of any happiness there, or they simply don't realize they're dead because they died so suddenly and unexpectedly. Some land in a dark place on the astral plane because of their fear and confusion and stay there a while until they're ready to experience themselves differently.

Your general state of consciousness or the state of consciousness at death determines what you will experience most immediately when you cross over to the astral plane. The different places, or "mansions," on the astral plane represent different states of consciousness, and people tend to go to a place that matches or reflects their general state of consciousness. This can change, of course, once they undergo more healing and their consciousness shifts to a higher, more light-filled state. Then, their experience of the astral plane becomes more joyful. Any experience is possible on the astral plane, and no one is doomed to any particular place. You choose where you are, in a sense, by choosing your state of consciousness, although this is rarely a conscious choice.

For this reason, the various "mansions" are often inhabited by like-minded souls, that is, people who have similar belief systems, since your beliefs or lack thereof determine your state of consciousness. Consequently, there are religious heavens, so to speak, which aren't very heavenly but are inhabited by those with similar religious views, who continue living out these views. In these cases, a "savior" might arrive periodically to try to help free these individuals from their limiting belief systems, which is one way people eventually move on from these so-called heavens.

I would be remiss if I didn't mention the wondrous possibilities of those who are unfettered by negativity on the astral plane. Once the disembodied are freed from their fear, guilt, anger, and other negativity around their death and previous lifetime, they're allowed to create and have all manner of experiences simply by choosing to have a particular experience.

On the astral plane, you can experience and explore anything you'd like, and you learn from these experiences, just as you do in your incarnations. People often choose to create lovely homes and environments and express their creativity in other ways. Some compose music, others paint, some study various subjects, while others teach, heal, and help others in various ways. The time in between lifetimes is another lifetime in a sense, one much freer and more carefree once you've overcome any blocks to experiencing the love and freedom that's available there.

There are many angels, guides, and discarnates available to assist those who are new to the astral plane. And, as you've so often heard, there's nearly always a loving, welcome committee of family members and friends eager to assist new arrivals in feeling at home.

Knowing all of this, I hope that at death you'll be able to set aside all fears of death and know that you'll be lovingly guided throughout, no matter what your state of consciousness. May this knowledge further shore up your resolve to be positive and live in a higher state of consciousness so that you have the easiest and most positive transition possible.

Ending One's Life

Suicide

This is a sensitive topic, and I will do my best to address it in a way that may, hopefully, bring some peace for all who struggle with the question of ending one's life.

There are many reasons people consider ending their life. Everyone who considers this believes they have good reason for this. Life has become too painful, either emotionally or physically. There's a feeling of not being able or willing to continue living the life they're living. Ending one's life seems like a way out of an untenable situation, one in which other alternatives seem lacking.

This is a particular mindset, of course, not the truth about any situation. No situation is untenable, even when there is a lot of physical pain. Human beings are able to endure large amounts of physical pain and often choose to rather than die, since the drive for survival is very strong. With *emotional* pain, however, this will to live is undermined by negative thoughts and feelings, which can make life feel unbearable. And, of course, physical pain is exacerbated by emotional pain in most cases, and in those cases, suicide may seem like the only option. And yet, many have learned to live with ongoing physical pain, and it might even be part of their life's purpose to explore this and perhaps help others to learn to deal with such pain.

Many things *feel* quite unbearable to the ego, as expressed in the voice in your head, and those feelings reinforce the belief that the situation actually *is* untenable. The mind spins a story about a situation, painting it as terrible and impossibly difficult, feelings follow from those thoughts, which further convince a person that the situation is impossible and hopeless. *Feelings* make a situation unbearable, not the actual situation but the feelings that stem from what people tell themselves about a situation. In this way, people dig themselves into emotional holes that are difficult to get out of. The only way out is for beliefs, or the stories they're telling themselves, to change, and changing one's beliefs isn't easy.

To change your beliefs, you have to be willing to examine them to see if they are true or faulty. The problem is that people don't naturally do this. Most don't realize that the beliefs they hold are faulty. They assume that their thoughts paint an accurate picture of reality and that they could feel no other way. They don't see that *they* created their inner experience of whatever they are going through by whatever they are telling themselves about it. Nevertheless, this is exactly what needs to be seen, what needs to be learned. This is one of the most important lessons in your human evolution, and it isn't an easy one to master. In your world, relatively few are even aware of this great truth: *You* create your experience of life.

One of the most important questions to ask in the examination of your thoughts is, "Where do these beliefs come from?" You might discover that they come from parents or someone else in your formative years, and that can be helpful. But the real question in terms of their origin is, Are these thoughts really yours? Did you choose to think them? Or are you what is aware of these thoughts arising out of nowhere? Until you have a greater awareness that your thoughts are not actually *yours* but your ego's—your programming—you will believe them and identify with them. You'll take ownership of them, and that's a problem.

These thoughts that originate from the ego are a problem because they build a case against life more often than they build a case *for* life. Why is that? Your thoughts, because they are mostly from your ego, have a negative view of life. They look out on the world and see lack, hardship, struggle, unhappiness, and pain. This is all the more true for those of you who grew up in an abusive household or who had parents who were deeply entrenched in their own egos and negativity. Perhaps they were depressed or otherwise living a life they didn't find fulfilling for whatever reason.

Everyone has the potential for such a negative outlook and extreme unhappiness and hopelessness by virtue of having an ego, but not everyone falls prey to this. Many have learned to overcome the negativity of the ego and to think more positively, and those who had parents who worked at being positive were fortunate indeed. Those who did not must work especially hard at overcoming not only their own ego but their parents' ego, you could say, as the psychology of one's parents often become one's own psychology.

But there is another force at work here, which must be named, that is not the ego but more nefarious. I don't wish to speak about this in any way that alarms or frightens you because this force, although negative, is not actually powerful, but it *is* real. There are negative forces that exist on other dimensions that do tamper with human beings, especially those who are already entrenched in negativity or addictions and leading unhappy lives.

Being in a state of negativity due to your own ego or to negative forces involved with those close to you, such as your parents, makes you vulnerable to negative forces. Fortunately, the only way they're able to influence you is through the voice in your head, as is the case with your own ego. Still, the negativity that they're able to implant in people's minds can be quite compelling and difficult to dismiss. Such negativity arouses your fight or flight mechanism, releasing chemicals into your system that convince you that something terrible is afoot, when it isn't.

"Sticks and stones can break your bones, but names will never hurt you." This childhood aphorism is a good one to remember when under attack by negative thoughts. Your negative thoughts cannot harm you or have any effect whatsoever—unless you believe them. Then, they do affect your system and potentially how you respond to others and to life.

Unfortunately, those who've grown up with a lot of negativity from parents do tend to believe such thoughts and believe them strongly and without question, and that's the problem. On the other hand, there are young people who grew up with happy and emotionally healthy parents who are still desperately unhappy and wish to end their lives. The social climate in your world coupled with violent video games and extremely disturbing images of violence in movies and TV are responsible for causing many young people to be overtaken by negativity, which their parents often feel powerless to do anything about.

What is behind such violence and ugliness in your world is the same thing that is behind the ugliness in one's psychological world: negative nonphysical entities. Many people are taken over by negativity without realizing that they're being affected by negative nonphysical entities. This is why I've often spoken of this phenomenon—not to frighten you but to inform you, because knowledge is power in this regard.

Knowing of this phenomenon empowers you to see that such entities need not have power over you or your world. Light must be shed on this darkness to dispel it, and so I do my best to name it. The darkness is powerless once brought to light. Negative entities are not particularly difficult to dispel, but they need to be acknowledged and sent on their way, into the Light, or they will linger and continue to affect people.

I mention this now because negative entities are involved in nearly all suicides. They instill and magnify the negative thoughts that make life so unbearable, and they plant the idea of suicide as the solution.

Life is not unbearable. Whatever emotions you feel are unbearable are, in fact, a mirage. If you are seeking to end your life because of how you feel emotionally, then this suffering is an opportunity to discover who you truly are and what cannot suffer, which is the goal of all your lifetimes. This is a tall order, but this is the role of suffering—to bring you back Home to the truth about who you really are and all that you are capable of: all the love, wisdom, compassion, and strength that is your true nature. Suffering is meant to bring out and help you cultivate your innate goodness and strengths. Suffering is not a reason to give up but a reason to become stronger in courage, compassion, patience, perseverance, and empathy.

Suffering is the greatest spiritual catalyst. Without it, people are unlikely to grow or likely to grow only very slowly. Often, the soul will choose circumstances that will result in suffering, such as an abusive early life or difficult early circumstances, to catapult the soul to a higher level of consciousness, to a greater awareness of who they really are. Although suffering doesn't always result in growth, the soul is often willing to take a chance that it will. Growth is that important to the soul. And certain kinds of growth, such as learning compassion or empathy cannot be gained any other way. As a result, all souls willingly choose difficult early environments and other challenges when that will serve. This is part of every soul's curriculum.

And because suffering is a necessary experience for everyone until it's mastered, or overcome, there's no point in trying to avoid it by ending your life. That will only delay your mastery of it. The soul will choose circumstances again in another lifetime to learn what needs to be learned. The tragedy of suicide is that it is a missed opportunity to grow, and that opportunity will have to be recreated another time. It's also a tragedy for those close to the one who committed suicide, for there are always people left behind who grieve such a loss, even in cases when that individual felt very alone. Everyone's life affects everyone else's. Each of you matters, and the loss of your life is a loss for life.

Suicide, although a loss of opportunity for the soul, is not a stain on the soul. I want to make this very clear. Those who commit suicide will not be met with punishment or judgment on the other side. Quite the contrary. They will be met, as all souls are, with great love and compassion and all the help they need to understand the life they recently left and learn from it.

Those who committed suicide will also receive healing, particularly emotional healing, since emotional pain and misunderstandings were the cause of their death. They'll be shown how they were mistaken in their perceptions and how they might have chosen differently. And they'll be shown how they affected others and how much those around them loved and cared for them. Abusive or insensitive parents love their children, even if they're unable to express that. They'll also be shown why others behaved badly toward them and that, under the circumstances, they weren't capable of behaving differently. In this way, they'll be helped to forgive others and forgive themselves, which is part of every healing process.

No, suffering is no reason to end your life or to fall into despair or regret. Suffering is an indication that you are believing something false, that you've fallen prey to negativity. The question is: How am I making myself suffer? If it's not possible to change your immediate situation, it's all the more important to change your attitude toward the situation. When you are caught between a rock and a hard place, you have to find a way to stay strong and stay positive. You must come to see that the alternative—to feel victimized, bitter, resentful, angry, or hateful—is not an acceptable option. You must learn to say no to such feelings and the stories that give birth to them. These are the ego's responses to difficulties, and these responses will only make your life more difficult.

It takes experience and maturity to see this, however, and some guidance from others is also very helpful. There is a way out of suffering, and everyone's challenge in life is to discover this for themselves. That is the hero's challenge, the dragon you must slay. The dragon is your negative thoughts and feelings. You are more than these thoughts and feelings, and to survive happily, you must come to see that you are more than the ego's knee-jerk responses to life. Those responses will only make you and everyone around you miserable.

Euthanasia

With euthanasia, I'm referring to steps taken to end one's life when there's nothing left to do to save it or nothing short of extreme measures that one is unwilling to undergo. Those in this situation need to check within and determine for themselves what seems right in their particular situation. It should be their choice whether to undergo extreme measures or not.

Because the medical establishment is pledged to do anything it can to extend life, people need to decide for themselves if what the medical establishment suggests is what they want. They need to be the ones to set the boundaries because the medical establishment will not. Because the person is the one who'll experience the consequences of that decision, the person must be the one to decide this.

The medical establishment isn't always right in how they see things and how they proceed. They see it as their responsibility to keep people alive at all costs, but that cost may be too great for the person and their family on several levels, and it may be more appropriate to allow someone to die rather than undergo extreme measures. It may be that person's time to go. Many do believe that there is such a thing as "one's time to go," but this isn't taken into account by the medical establishment, understandably.

End-of-life issues raise deep questions that society and individuals must grapple with. This is always a difficult place in a world's evolution, where there is technology that can save lives but little ethical understanding or agreement about how to apply this technology. This is one of the questions your world must answer: when to save a life and when not to, when to try to hold off death and when to yield to death. This is a question that must be answered for those with a critical illness as well as those born prematurely, and this is a very complex and individual decision.

Currently, the answer is to always try to save a life, but that isn't always the best choice for a soul. Some suffer unnecessarily when it's their time to go because they or those around them don't accept or understand that it's their time to go. Furthermore, interventions are being made to sustain the lives of, essentially, fetuses that are not ready to be born, many of which will have lasting effects if the child survives.

In the case of extreme premature birth, you could argue that the soul chose to have that experience and its consequences, and you would be right, as the soul can and will leave if it can't use that vehicle for growth. The soul is quite flexible, and it will find another body to incarnate into if the one intended is no longer available or suitable. Nevertheless, there is often great and unnecessary suffering involved in these cases on the part of the infant.

Although suffering is an important means of growth, suffering does not have to be sought if it can be avoided, particularly physical suffering at the end of life. Just as you humanely euthanize your pets when their bodies are failing, there's a place for euthanasia as a means of reducing physical suffering at the end of one's life. Euthanasia is for those who are suffering physically, as it is not an answer to emotional suffering, as I said earlier. The answer to emotional suffering isn't death but learning to live.

If people had a better understanding of death and weren't afraid of it, the end of life wouldn't be so difficult for so many. A general lack of understanding and fear of death is, in part, responsible for the extraordinary measures that people allow at the end of life, which make dying more difficult than it needs to be. If only there were a way to determine whether it was someone's time to go and people were not afraid to die. This would reduce the amount suffering for everyone immensely. But alas, those in your world who might be able to supply this information are sidelined and not respected—and who would want the responsibility of making such a pronouncement anyway? The situation is challenging indeed.

There will come a time when people will be comfortable with the idea of knowing that it's someone's time to go and allowing that to take place naturally or with assistance. In the meantime, everyone is doing their best with this issue and hoping they're making the right choices. Ultimately, the choices that are made don't matter, as the soul learns from every experience. Since that is true, perhaps the best guide is to do whatever is likely to have the best results with the least amount of suffering and also to assist people in dying in the way they choose if they're unwilling to take further measures to extend their life.

In their later years, many decline slowly over a number of years without any life-threatening condition. When this is the case, then that's the right experience, and the soul can gain immensely from such an experience, although it may take many lifetimes of dying in this way before the soul learns what is intended. What can be gained by slowly losing one's abilities is a realization that what you are has little to do with the body. Who you essentially are is untouched by what the body is experiencing.

This is also one of the lessons, if not the main lesson, in debilitating illnesses. By noticing what remains when the body no longer functions and you aren't able to do the things that gave you a particular identity, who are you? You never really were any of your roles or any of your accomplishments, and this is plainly seen, as what remains shines through, untouched by the body's experience. This is one of the more difficult lessons, as it requires an enormous amount of surrender, but once that is accomplished, even this challenge can result in joy and a great appreciation for the gift of life.

Conclusion

Once you are beyond this life and have undergone any necessary healing of trauma and mistaken beliefs and come to peace with the life you just left, the afterlife is free of suffering and full of joy. The suffering you experience as a human being is a function of your human ego, and that same ego doesn't exist in the afterlife.

In the afterlife, your personality might be similar to the one you had or a combination of personalities from former lifetimes. Your personality is much more flexible and positive than it was when you were human. You can also choose how you'll appear, including your age. You can choose to appear as you did in some other lifetime or however you wish, and you can change your appearance as often as you like.

The afterlife is a time of learning. Your soul learns a great deal from the choices it makes in the afterlife just as it did when you were human, but you aren't confined to the limitations you were as a human. You can explore much more freely and fully than you could as a human.

Why? Because that's the nature of spirit. It's only because you were human that you were limited and experienced the negative thoughts and emotions you did. This negativity is gone in the afterlife. You are happy.

That's not to say that there aren't those who are unhappy in the afterlife, for a soul can choose to be unhappy, and some do, to punish themselves for having behaved badly on earth. Some suffer greatly for a time, but that's their choice. Suffering is not imposed on any soul for any reason. For a time, a soul is allowed to choose suffering, all the while being encouraged to let that go and learn from one's mistakes. Even *self*-punishment doesn't serve the soul, but that's just one more lesson to be learned.

In the afterlife, there's such freedom because your natural state as spirit is free! If you were God (and you are), wouldn't you give yourself freedom? Freedom is the natural outgrowth of love for oneself and for life. Freedom is integral to happiness, and happiness is an outgrowth of the love that is at your core.

Happiness *is* love, and love *is* happiness. This is your birthright, and you are only playing in a world of challenge and negativity for your soul's exploration, expansion—and yes—enjoyment, because there *is* enjoyment in such exploration and expansion even when this is challenging.

You, as a human being, may not experience that joy in the midst of difficulties, although it's always there in your being. But because the soul's perspective includes what is gained from an experience, the soul is in joy even in the midst of challenges. Perhaps the learning will come only after many lifetimes, but that's no problem for the soul. It knows that the end result of all your experiences is greater love and joy, and that's its goal.

In these pages, we have seen how the soul uses tragedies and other challenges to make you stronger, wiser, more patient, more compassionate, and more accepting. These rewards make the challenges worthwhile. Even the challenges, themselves, don't have to be so difficult if you can bring these things—strength, wisdom, patience, compassion, and acceptance—to them.

Conclusion

What a benefit it is to know this! I do hope that your life is made easier and more joyful as a result of the understanding presented here. It is my deepest wish that you know your true nature as spirit, to the extent that you can as a human being, and that you have great compassion for your humanness. This will bring you peace amidst your human trials. You are so much more than a human being!

Appendix

The Astrological Signs

Keep in mind that everyone has many different signs in their chart that shape the personality and one's expression, not just the Sun's sign. Of greatest importance in addition to the Sun's sign is the Moon's sign, the Ascendant, Venus's sign, Mars' sign, and Mercury's sign.

ARIES

Arians are independent, strong, courageous, pioneering, assertive, and enterprising. They take the lead in initiating activities and new ventures, although they are not known for following through on their projects. For this, they usually depend on others. They are leaders in whatever field they are found but especially excel in fields that utilize their courage, initiative, and competitive drive. Athletics, the military, car racing, police work, firefighting, emergency work, and crisis intervention are examples, but science and other enterprises that require a pioneering spirit are other possibilities. Many are mechanically inclined.

Cooperation is not their strong suit, since Arians tend to be focused on their own needs and drives. Their relationships often suffer as a result, but this is also true of the other fire signs—Leo and Sagittarius. Arians need to learn to listen to others, to cooperate, to slow down, to think before they act, and to be patient. Failure to do these things results in conflict, accidents, and wasted energy. Arians tend to burn-out, since they are so action-oriented. Consequently, they can benefit from more introspection and planning. They are happiest when they are moving and taking action toward their goals, however. They are somewhat suspect of those who are overly intellectual, as they believe in living spontaneously, by their wits and wills.

Arians love excitement, the outdoors, activity, physical exertion, adventure, risk-taking, challenge, and competition. They do not mind conflict in the least, and often invite it by their actions. This disturbs more sensitive and accommodating signs, who are taken aback by their brazenness and boldness. Arians, however, are not at all disturbed by others' reactions to them, which is one reason they do not learn easily about relationships.

Needs: freedom, independence, initiative, self-assertion, discovery, leadership, to pioneer, to protect the weak, to champion a cause, to be first

Positive expression: initiating, pioneering, enterprising, direct, straightforward, spontaneous, self-directed, self-motivated, self-reliant, independent, individualistic, confident, a leader, risk-taking, courageous, active, energetic, dynamic, outgoing, assertive, confrontative, passionate, creative, inspiring, expressive

Negative expression: impulsive, hasty, impatient, lacks follow-through, headstrong, pushy, uncooperative, rash, reckless, careless, foolhardy, competitive, domineering, restless, overactive, aggressive, argumentative, combative, pushy, quick-tempered, egocentric, self-absorbed

Needs to learn: patience, cooperation, conservation of energy, completion

TAURUS

Taureans are hard-working, persevering, slow to react, conservative, practical, materialistic, and attached to routine. It is perhaps because they are creatures of habit and don't mind the day-to-day grind others find monotonous that they are able to achieve as much as they do. Taureans accomplish a great deal because they are masters of the material realm. They know how to make their way in the world. The desire for security is one of their motivations.

Taureans are also motivated by their love for comfort and beauty. Many surround themselves with beauty and indulge themselves with the sensual delights as a reward for their efforts in the world. Taureans are sensual beings in every sense of the word and tend to disbelieve anything that cannot be experienced through their senses. They, therefore, may lack a spiritual perspective and distrust their intuition.

While Taureans are known for their ability to get things done, they are also known for their stubbornness and inflexibility, the flip-side of their perseverance. Their inflexibility gets them into trouble in relationships, which often call for adaptability, especially during times of transition. Taureans act as if life should not change, when the opposite is true. Despite this,

Taureans have a sweet, gentle, easygoing personality and a stability many rely on.

Because of their love of beauty, Taureans are often found in the arts or businesses related to beauty or the production of beautiful things. They also may be found in businesses related to sensual pleasures, like massage or the sale of food, liquor, wine, or sweets. Many also are attracted to professions that deal with finances, since they have such a knack for and interest in money. And finally, because Taurus is an earth sign, many pursue professions related to the earth or products of the earth, such as farming, geology, gardening, or landscape architecture.

Needs: sensual pleasures, beauty, comfort, security, money and material possessions, to be productive

Positive expression: loyal, affectionate, practical, honors tradition, conserving, self-sufficient, productive, hard-working, knows how to make money, resourceful, managerial, patient, persistent, strong-willed, determined, stable, steady, reliable, artistic, easygoing, gentle, sensual, pleasure-loving

Negative expression: possessive, jealous, attached, acquisitive, materialistic, stingy, greedy, security-oriented, ultraconservative, conformist, conventional, unoriginal, unspiritual, slow, plodding, stubborn, obstinate, unchanging, dull, boring, lazy, self-indulgent, hedonistic, gluttonous

Needs to learn: detachment, flexibility, a true sense of values

GEMINI

Geminis are sociable, versatile, dexterous, adaptable, quick, and verbally and mentally active. They are never short on conversation or ideas, as they thrive on both. Gemini is the sign of communication and all this entails. They are teachers, news reporters, editors, writers, librarians, secretaries, and students of the world. They are drawn to occupations that relate to the accumulation and dissemination of knowledge. Their curiosity is insatiable.

Geminis have a lightheartedness, friendliness, and wit about them, which endears them to others and wins them popularity. However, they are not known for intimacy or commitment, perhaps because their independence, restlessness, and appreciation for all kinds of people is so great. They are very tolerant of differences in people, which they find intriguing.

Their curiosity and interest in people propel them from place to place and experience to experience. They are the butterflies of the zodiac. However, in their explorations, they may fail to grasp the larger picture. Much of their investigation of life tends to be superficial, unfocused, and aimless. This is not necessarily bad, but it may prevent them from accomplishing anything substantial. A Gemini lifetime is often for the purpose of gathering information and experiences, which can be put into some kind of order or understanding later in their evolution or just later in life.

Geminis sometimes have a problem being too adaptable, too mutable. They are like chameleons, imitating and going along with whoever and whatever is around them. This may prevent them from pursuing their own goals, as they are so easily lost in the moment. And because they are so adaptable and able to see the good in any situation, they may stay in negative situations too long. On the other hand, they may change courses too easily, whenever the going gets tough, and not benefit from the challenges they are faced with. Because they enjoy change and variety, they may opt for changing their outer circumstances rather than growing inwardly.

Needs: to know, to learn, to communicate, to teach, to write, to move about, to make contact with people and the environment

Positive expression: adaptable, versatile, jack of all trades, many interests, lively, agile, quick, alert, dexterous, sociable, congenial, tolerant, curious, logical, rational, scientific, knowledgeable, verbal, articulate, eloquent, clever, amusing, witty

Negative expression: scattered, dabbling, superficial, two-faced, changeable, unreliable, uncommitted, fickle, ambivalent, inconsistent, flighty, nervous, restless, high-strung, lacking concentration, involved with trivia, imitative, overly logical, rationalizing, unfeeling, detached, shallow, unphilosophical, lacking purpose or depth of understanding, talks too much, chit chats, gossipy, manipulative, cunning, dishonest

Needs to learn: discrimination, to focus the mind

CANCER

Cancers are sensitive, sweet, kind, intuitive, compassionate, and dependent. They live for home, family, and community. They thrive on emotional closeness and attachment. Cancers need to give love and to be needed as much as they need love, which makes them ideal caretakers of others. Cancer lifetimes increase one's ability to love and care for others. However, because Cancers are so focused on their nurturing relationships and on other people's feelings and needs, they may neglect their own needs and identity. This can cause them to feel resentful and bitter and is one reason they are known for being moody or "crabby."

The other reason they are moody is that they are so sensitive to the energies around them. They pick up on other people's feelings and feel them. This is an advantage in being able to empathize and care for others, but a disadvantage to their own health and well-being. They need to learn to discriminate between other people's feelings and their own and to protect themselves from the negativity around them. They also need to learn to assert their own needs if they are to serve others joyfully. And finally, they need to learn objectivity, since their feelings can be overwhelming at times.

Cancers are security-minded, conservative and oriented toward the past. They enjoy history, tradition, antiques, genealogy, archeology, and anything old. They are often nostalgic and sentimental, and may have difficulty letting go of the past. Cancers are the ones who carry on the family traditions and hold the family together.

Cancers are attracted to the helping professions, to the food and hotel industries, to work related to children or caretaking, to real estate, to work involving domestic products or services, and to professions that require imagination such as writing.

Needs: to give and receive nurturing, roots, home, family, financial and emotional security

Positive expression: maternal, nurturing, protective, nourishing, helpful, sensitive, soft-hearted, deeply feeling, psychic, intuitive, loyal, devoted, tenacious, domestic, family-oriented, honors the past, self-protective, reserved, cautious, thrifty, conservative

Negative expression: smothering, suffocating, possessive, overly emotional, moody, hypersensitive, easily hurt, maudlin, overly sentimental, overly impressionable, needy, loses self in others, clinging, parasitic, dependent, passive, clannish, stay-at-home, provincial, clings to the past, secretive, withdrawn, martyr, self-pitying

Needs to learn: objectivity, independence

LEO

Leos are fun-loving, playful, warm, creative, and expressive. They give of themselves exuberantly, but on their own terms. They thrive on leadership, and seek to order and control circumstances and people around them. Besides being natural leaders, they are natural teachers, since they love the attention that goes with being an authority. In their role as leader and teacher, they can be dramatic, persuasive, spellbinding, and irresistible. Part of their charm is their courage, enthusiasm, and outgoing drive.

Because of their determination, Leos are hard to disagree with and hard to stop once their minds are set on something. They have no trouble convincing others that they are right, because they are so convinced themselves. Their confidence is contagious, which is one reason for their popularity and following. Leos command respect because they demand it and because they believe in themselves.

APPENDIX: THE ASTROLOGICAL SIGNS

Unfortunately, they can be egotistical, arrogant, and domineering. With the good qualities of Leo come some bad ones, such as the need for control and insensitivity to the ideas and needs of others. Leos don't mean to run roughshod over others; they are just so certain of their own beliefs and goals that they don't let others delay or dissuade them. Consequently, relationships can be a challenge for them. They need to learn to be flexible, to share power with others, and to cooperate. They also need to learn to lead with compassion and with the good of the whole in mind, for sometimes they can be power-hungry and self-serving.

Leo is often found in the charts of those developing talent in the performance arts. Their creativity and drive for self-expression often lead them into entertainment professions or other fields that cater to an audience. They are also attracted to professions involving recreation, sports, amusements, games, toys, and children. Business management is another area in which they excel.

Needs: ego expansion, independence, recognition, authority, admiration, leadership, self-expression, creativity, love

Positive expression: confident, self-assured, strong, independent, dignified, charismatic, capable of managing and leading, commanding, powerful, determined, strong-willed, generous, benevolent, magnanimous, affectionate, warm, loyal, faithful, romantic, playful, spontaneous, fun-loving, entertaining, dramatic, creative, self-expressive

Negative expression: egocentric, self-important, arrogant, snobbish, dominating, power-mad, overbearing, bossy, extravagant, indulgent, womanizing, needs excessive love and admiration, self-indulgent, childish, incapable of being serious, melodramatic, show-off, ostentatious, must be the center of attention

Needs to learn: humility, cooperation, adaptability

VIRGO

Virgos are humble, efficient, and dedicated workers. They need to feel useful. Because they place work and service above all else, other aspects of their lives sometimes suffer, particularly their personal lives. On a personal level, Virgos are reserved, shy, and cool emotionally. They shun undue attention or limelight. They do, however, enjoy people and thrive on helping them, which they do in a way that is unassuming and with little expectation of return except the satisfaction of service. However, Virgos sometimes serve even when they don't want to, which can result in their feeling bitter, resentful, and oppressed. Virgos are learning to serve joyfully. Giving to others is, after all, the greatest pleasure of all. This is what Virgo lifetimes teach.

Virgos are known for their ability to handle details. Consequently, they make excellent secretaries, bookkeepers, librarians, writers, computer programmers, researchers, analysts, surgeons, draftspersons, technicians, mathematicians, repairmen, craftsmen, and editors. They excel at any profession that demands careful attention to detail, thoroughness, organization, and efficiency. Virgos are perfectionists, which makes them valuable workers, although their perfectionism can be difficult for them and others to live with. They need to learn to be gentle with themselves.

And finally, because Virgo is the sign of health and healing, many Virgos find themselves in the healing professions, where they can use their drive to help others, their attention to detail, their keen intellect, and their strong practical capabilities and common sense. Virgo lifetimes emphasize work and service; and Virgos, along with the other earth signs, Taurus and Capricorn, perform the bulk of the practical work needed by society.

Needs: to be efficient and useful, serve, heal others, analyze, discriminate, organize, attend to details, do things well

Positive expression: exacting, methodical, detail-oriented, orderly, organized, meticulous, systematic, efficient, diligent, industrious, thorough, devoted to work and service, responsible, dependable, conscientious, studious, mentally sharp, discriminating, analytical, modest, unassuming, humble, helpful, health-conscious

Negative expression: picky, finicky, petty, fussy, overly fastidious, perfectionistic, always busy, workaholic, cannot relax, hypercritical, self-critical, nagging, intolerant, prudish, overly analytical, worrying, anxious, negative, complaining, timid, self-deprecating, servile, subservient, submissive, hypochondriac, food fanatic

Needs to learn: tolerance of imperfections in oneself and others, lightheartedness

LIBRA

Libras are one of the more sociable signs. They are sweet, kind, considerate, helpful, and polite. They thrive on relationships, particularly one-to-one relationships. In fact, Libras are not happy when they are not in a special relationship or partnership.

For most Libras, partnership and its lessons—sharing, negotiating, compromising, giving, and getting along with others—are integral to their spiritual growth. As a result, Libras often bend backwards to please others, sometimes at the expense of their own needs and dreams.

Their most common fault is giving up their identity for someone else or never finding one. This is neither true giving nor true relationship. A lifetime as a Libra can be a real balancing act between I and thou, with the thou usually winning out. Consequently, Libras often benefit from classes in assertiveness and encouragement to pursue their own goals and dreams separate from their partner's.

Balance is a key word for Libras. They strive for harmony, beauty, peace, and balance in everything they do. Therefore, when making decisions, they are objective, thoughtful, and rational. The problem is that, in being able to see all sides of a question, they have a terrible time making decisions. On the other hand, this objectivity and fairness makes them good negotiators, mediators, counselors, and peacemakers, roles they often find themselves in. They are generous, kind, and forgiving of others, which is why they are so good at teaching others how to get along.

Their strong relationship skills make them natural counselors and mediators. They also are often drawn to the law profession because of their idealism and strong sense of justice. The arts, design, or decoration are other areas that appeal to them, because they can exercise their love for beauty, sense of balance, and aesthetic sense. Professions requiring charm, diplomacy, politeness, beauty, and refinement also suit them.

Needs: partnership, beauty, balance, justice, harmony, peace

Positive expression: relationship-oriented, sociable, cooperating, mediating, pleasing, agreeable, likeable, charming, hospitable, diplomatic, tactful, peace-loving, harmonious, poised, elegant, refined, artistic, good taste, strong aesthetic sense, cultured, beauty-conscious, sees all sides, fair, just, idealistic

Negative expression: other-oriented, dependent, overly accommodating, placating, compliant, overemphasizing appearances, vain, superficial, vacillating, indecisive, unable to accept reality

Needs to learn: decisiveness, independence, self-assertion

SCORPIO

Scorpio, like Libra, is a sign of relationship, but Scorpios' involvement in relationships is intense and power-oriented. Scorpios are emotional, secretive, reserved, passionate, intense, determined, and goal-oriented. They know what they want and pursue it relentlessly even if it means going against someone else. Like Libra, Scorpio has lessons regarding sharing, negotiating, cooperating, and being an equal partner. However, Scorpios are the ones in the relationship who tend not to do these things. And yet, they crave relationship as intensely as Libras and therefore must learn to do these things.

Scorpios are deep. They are interested in the mysterious and hidden aspects of life. It is not surprising that they often are drawn to research, detective work, psychology, and metaphysics. They demand depth, intensity, and emotional intimacy from their relationships as well, which tend to be dependent, enmeshed, and possessive.

Their tenacity is one of their strengths when applied to the right area. Scorpios are able to accomplish tremendous feats because of their strong will, endurance, and perseverance. However, their inflexibility often results in power conflicts and difficulty navigating life's transitions. Although Scorpios have intense and deep emotions, they are reserved and secretive about their feelings. They also are highly intuitive and live from their feelings and intuitions.

Scorpios are interested in both personal and societal transformation, and often work in fields that bring about this transformation. Some examples are the healing arts, hypnotherapy, past life regression therapy, psychology, spiritual healing, psychic work, channeling, recycling, urban renovation, and political activism. They are attracted to professions involving life or death matters, hidden or unknown aspects of life, research, rebuilding or renewal, deep emotional probing, intense interactions with others, crisis intervention, and emergency work.

Needs: self-mastery, power, control, self-transformation, intimacy, to explore and uncover what is hidden or esoteric, psychological and metaphysical understanding

Positive expression: deeply feeling, intense, passionate, strong, courageous, loyal, effective in emergencies, determined, strong-willed, persevering, self-disciplined, self-controlled, thorough, penetrating, probing, investigating, resourceful, profound, insightful, magnetic, mysterious, self-protective, reserved, capable of psychological and spiritual transformation

Negative expression: overly intense, morbid, brooding, lustful, violent, possessive, jealous, unforgiving, resentful, revengeful, willful, unyielding, obsessive, controlling, extremist, ruthless, manipulative, scheming, exploitative, secretive, cruel, destructive, subversive, judgmental, repressed

Needs to learn: forgiveness, letting go, sharing, correct use of power

SAGITTARIUS

Sagittarians are generous, happy-go-lucky, fun-loving, outgoing, exuberant, adventuresome, independent, and optimistic — sometimes too much so. Their faults are their good qualities taken to the extreme. Thus, they can be foolhardy, grandiose, extravagant, arrogant, self-centered, unrealistic, and irresponsible. Nevertheless, they are very likeable and never mean to be insensitive or unkind. However, relationships are not their forte.

Because Sagittarians thrive on freedom and adventure, they don't necessarily do well in relationships nor do they need them as much as many of the other signs. Sagittarian lifetimes are more involved with learning, teaching, and exploring than with close, personal relationships.

Sagittarians are seekers. Because they seek adventure and excitement, they love to travel. And because they seek understanding and wisdom, they love to read and study. However they never seek knowledge for its own sake, but for a higher purpose. They are philosophers, professors, sages, gurus, and priests, who seek to uncover the nature of human existence. They are truth seekers and teachers.

Faith is a key word for Sagittarius. Sagittarians need to believe in something and they need to have goals. A Sagittarian without a vision or without the freedom to pursue that vision is a sad sight indeed. Sagittarian lifetimes are truly ones of seeking—and discovering—meaning and a higher purpose.

Sagittarians are found in higher education, the legal profession, the ministry, publishing, lecturing, writing, editing, astrology, metaphysics, the import/export business, foreign trade, and the travel industry. They are explorers, adventurers, athletes, vagabonds, and astronauts.

Needs: independence, freedom, growth, improvement, goals, understanding, meaning, philosophy or belief system, travel, exploration

Positive expression: purposeful, goal-directed, aspiring, seeking meaning and understanding, philosophical, having faith, optimistic, prophetic, future-oriented, idealistic, open-minded, self-improving, wise, profound, discerning, enlightened, well-read, inspirational, guiding, teaching, ethical, principled, generous, openhearted, direct, frank, truthful, likeable, jovial, enthusiastic, happy-go-lucky, carefree, exploring, freedom-loving, outdoorsy

Negative expression: impractical, unrealistic, blindly optimistic, overly abstract, didactic, long-winded, dogmatic, moralistic, intolerant, preachy, hypocritical, blunt, tactless, outspoken, wasteful, extravagant, exaggerating, careless, irresponsible, unreliable, overextended, restless, wanderlust, cannot tolerate restrictions

Needs to learn: tolerance, moderation, sensitivity, tact, responsibility

CAPRICORN

As is true of all the signs next to each other in the zodiac, Sagittarius and Capricorn are opposite in many ways. Capricorns are cautious, serious, realistic, reliable, persevering, practical, responsible, materialistic, hard-working, conservative, and tend toward pessimism. Both Sagittarians and Capricorns, however, are concerned about society's structures. Sagittarians are concerned with the law, ethics, morals, and philosophies that underlie society, while Capricorns are concerned with building and maintaining the structures or institutions of society. This is why many Capricorns in capitalistic societies are business executives or administrators. Many also are found in government or politics, or other positions of authority in society.

Capricorns care very much about their social position and career. They are determined to get to the top in whatever profession they are in. Rarely are they happy settling for second best. They live to work and be recognized in what they do. They never shirk their responsibilities and are always reliable. Consequently, Capricorns often do excel in their careers and achieve high honors. They prefer positions of leadership, and their strong ambition and initiative usually get them there.

This dedication to work and material security can take its toll on their personal relationships and family life, however, which is something Capricorns often have to work at. Capricorns often look for a partner who will take care of the personal, emotional side of life for them so that they won't have to deal with these things. However, the personal side of life cannot be escaped or ignored, which is where their lessons come in. Capricorns need to learn to be more sociable, trusting, playful, optimistic, lighthearted, kind, and spontaneous.

Needs: structure, control, leadership, responsibility, achievement, power, recognition, status, security

Positive expression: serious, fatherly, earnest, reserved, realistic, practical, thrifty, cautious, prudent, controlled, self-disciplined, self-sufficient, self-reliant, stoical, persistent, persevering, responsible, reliable, scrupulous, dutiful, adheres to rules, diligent, hard-working, achieving, ambitious, enterprising, successful, powerful, managerial, executive capability

Negative expression: pessimistic, gloomy, brooding, cynical, materialistic, stingy, fearful, distrustful, overly cautious, closed, repressed, inhibited, rigid, misanthropic, insensitive, cruel, cold, harsh, conservative, ultra-conventional, obsessed with rules/formalities, perfectionistic, status-seeking, power-hungry, calculating, authoritarian, domineering, exploitative

Needs to learn: sociability, kindness, flexibility, lightheartedness

AQUARIUS

Aquarians are friendly but aloof, tolerant, objective, intellectual, inventive, original, progressive, humanitarian, individualistic, independent, freedom-loving, and future-oriented. They enjoy ideas and social interactions, especially ones that inspire them to think along new lines. Aquarians are the ones who bring new ideas to society. They are on the cutting edge and, consequently, often on the fringes of society. Sometimes Aquarians are so unusual, rebellious, and unconventional that they cannot function within society or find inroads in society for their ideas. These Aquarians may wind up feeling unfulfilled and bitter, for despite their independence and eccentricity, they do want to make a difference in the world.

Aquarians are friendly and sociable but not intimate. They are emotionally cool and detached. Aquarians have difficulty with intimacy, not only because they lead with their heads instead of their hearts, but also because they value their independence so highly. Independence allows them to pursue their unique ideas and visions for the future, which is what they value above all else. Although Aquarians are not at their best one-on-one, they value friendships highly and often thrive in groups, both benefitting from them and contributing significantly to them. They are particularly drawn to humanitarian groups or ones that seek to improve conditions for the earth and its creatures.

Aquarius is found in the charts of inventors, innovators, mathematicians, progressive thinkers, environmentalists, humanitarians, scientists, social workers, revolutionaries, social reformers, metaphysicians, psychics, astrologers, and new age thinkers. It is also related to new technology, electronics, broadcast media, engineering, and computers. Many Aquarians find themselves involved in group-related activities: seminars, workshops, clubs, teams, or professions that depend on group efforts. They are also futurists, science fiction writers, and in the space industry.

Needs: brotherhood, freedom, independence, individualism, group involvement, equality, friendship, community, new knowledge, change, to invent, to reform

Positive expression: intellectual, scientific, friendly, humanitarian, kind, tolerant, open-minded, unprejudiced, progressive, reformist, idealistic, politically active, independent, individualistic, unconventional, innovative, inventive, original, unique, unusual, intuitive, determined, strong will

Negative expression: coolly logical, impersonal, detached, aloof, remote, radical, revolutionary, utopian, impractical, rebellious, contrary, unpredictable, erratic, eccentric, bizarre, shocking, intolerant of rules and restraint, lawless, uncommitted

Needs to learn: to be intimate and personal

PISCES

Pisceans, like Aquarians, are humanitarian, visionary, and idealistic, but here the similarity ends. Pisces, being a water sign, is emotional, sensitive, warm, relationship-oriented, and receptive. Pisceans are known for their compassion, imagination, creativity, intuition, desire to serve, and devotion to God or higher ideals. They are also known for being ungrounded, unrealistic, impractical, spacey, unreliable, careless, and dependent.

Pisceans have difficulty functioning in the world, and yet their gift is attunement to other worlds. Many have an uncanny sensitivity to other people's energy and emotions. However, spiritual development is needed to know what to do with all this sensitivity. For some, life is simply too difficult to bear, and they retreat into their own world of imagination, drugs or alcohol, or depression. Pisceans need to learn to cope with and use their sensitivity so that they can serve others with it.

Service is a key word for Pisces. They need to serve. Without such a higher purpose, they are lost. However, because they care so deeply about other people and their needs, they often lose touch with or devalue their own needs. This can lead to emotional difficulties, resentment, and depression. They need to learn to identify, value, and assert their own needs before they will be truly ready to serve in the highest way. They also need a spiritual philosophy that will help them cope with being in the world and with the injustices they see around them.

Pisceans are found in the helping professions, particularly those related to mental health, such as psychiatric nursing, psychotherapy, hospice care, nursing home work, alcohol and drug counseling, or social work. They are also found in the arts. Many write romance novels or poetry, compose music, dance, and perform or create in other ways. They use their intuition and psychic abilities as astrologers, tarot readers, palmists, and healers. Some join religious orders. And some study metaphysics, yoga, meditation, Eastern religions, and dreams.

Needs: transcendence, serenity, spirituality, ideal love, beauty, emotional closeness, privacy, to serve others

Positive expression: flexible, going with the flow, surrendering, agreeable, easy to please, mellow, accepting, tolerant, forgiving, trusting, gentle, kind, sensitive, psychic, intuitive, sympathetic, compassionate, unselfish, giving, sacrificing, devotional, humble, unpretentious, introspective, imaginative, creative, inspired, musical, poetic, spiritual, transcendent, inspirational, mystical, idealistic, visionary

Negative expression: directionless, lost, easily influenced, overly impressionable, undiscriminating, soft, weak, submissive, unassertive, timid, easily hurt, oversensitive, martyr, overly sacrificing, dependent, parasitic, meek, cowardly, weak-willed, self-deprecating, self-pitying, easily victimized, evasive, indirect, devious, deceptive, escapist, daydreaming, impractical, unrealistic, deluded, spacey, confused, drug or alcohol addicted

Needs to learn: responsibility, perseverance, independence, self-assertion

About the Author

Gina Lake is a nondual spiritual teacher and the author of more than twenty books about awakening to one's true nature. She is also a gifted intuitive and channel with a master's degree in Counseling Psychology and over thirty years' experience supporting people in their spiritual growth. In 2012, Jesus began dictating books through her. These teachings from Jesus are based on universal truth, not on any religion.

Then in 2017, at the request of Jesus, Gina and her husband, who is also a nondual spiritual teacher, began offering Christ Consciousness Transmissions to groups online in weekly meetings and monthly intensives. These energy transmissions are a direct current of love and healing that accelerate one's spiritual evolution.

Gina's YouTube channel has over 250 messages from Jesus to listen to. Her website offers information about her books, online courses, transmissions, a free ebook, and audio and video recordings:

www.RadicalHappiness.com

Christ Consciousness Transmission (CCT) Online Weekly Meetings

Transmission is something that naturally happens from spiritual teacher to aspirant and from beings on higher dimensions to those who are willing to receive on this dimension. Transmission has been used throughout the ages to accelerate spiritual evolution and raise consciousness. In the process, emotional and sometimes physical healing also take place, as a clearing of energy blocks from the energy field is a necessary and natural part of raising consciousness.

In weekly online Zoom video meetings, Gina Lake and her husband offer Christ Consciousness transmissions. This is one of the ways that Jesus and the other Ascended Masters working with Jesus intend to raise humanity's level of consciousness. A channeled message from Jesus is given before the transmission to prepare, teach, and inspire those who are there to receive the transmission. Many report feeling a transmission come through these channeled messages as well.

The transmission takes around twenty minutes and is done in silence except for some music, which is meant to help people open and receive. During the transmission, Gina Lake and her husband are simply acting as antennas for Christ Consciousness, as it streams to earth to be received by all who are willing to open to and be uplifted by divine grace. Since there is actually no such thing as time and space, these are not a barrier to receiving the transmission, which works as well online as in person. You can find out more about these transmissions on Gina's website at:

www.RadicalHappiness.com/transmissions

If you enjoyed this book, we think you will also enjoy these other books from Jesus by Gina Lake...

What Jesus Wants You to Know Today: About Himself, Christianity, God, the World, and Being Human: Jesus exists and has always existed to serve humanity, and one way he is doing this today is through this channel, Gina Lake, and others. In *What Jesus Wants You to Know Today,* Jesus answers many questions about his life and teachings and shares his perspective on the world. He brings his message of love, once again, to the world and corrects the record by detailing the ways that Christianity has distorted his teachings. He wants you to know that you, too, have the potential to be a Christ, to be enlightened as he was, and he explains how this is possible.

The Jesus Trilogy. In this trilogy by Jesus, are three jewels, each shining in its own way and illuminating the same truth: You are not only human but divine, and you are meant to flourish and love one another. In words that are for today, Jesus speaks intimately and directly to the reader of the secrets to peace, love, and happiness. He explains the deepest of all mysteries: who you are and how you can live as he taught long ago. The three books in *The Jesus Trilogy* were dictated to Gina Lake by Jesus and include *Choice and Will, Love and Surrender,* and *Beliefs, Emotions, and the Creation of Reality.*

Awakening Now Online Course

It's time to start living what you've been reading about. Are you interested in delving more deeply into the teachings in Gina Lake's books, receiving ongoing support for waking up, and experiencing the power of Christ Consciousness transmissions? You'll find that and much more in the Awakening Now online course:

This course was created for your awakening. The methods presented are powerful companions on the path to enlightenment and true happiness. Awakening Now will help you experience life through fresh eyes and discover the delight of truly being alive. This 100-day inner workout is packed with both time-honored and original practices that will pull the rug out from under your ego and wake you up. You'll immerse yourself in materials, practices, guided meditations, and inquiries that will transform your consciousness. And in video webinars, you'll receive transmissions of Christ Consciousness. These transmissions are a direct current of love and healing that will accelerate your evolution and help you break through to a new level of being. By the end of 100 days, you will have developed new habits and ways of being that will result in being more richly alive and present and greater joy and equanimity.

www.RadicalHappiness.com/online-courses

More Books by Gina Lake

Available in paperback, ebook, and audiobook formats.

A Heroic Life: New Teachings from Jesus on the Human Journey. The hero's journey—this human life—is a search for the greatest treasure of all: the gifts of your true nature. These gifts are your birthright, but they have been hidden from you, kept from you by the dragon: the ego. These gifts are the wisdom, love, peace, courage, strength, and joy that reside at your core. *A Heroic Life* shows you how to overcome the ego's false beliefs and face the ego's fears. It provides you with both a perspective and a map to help you successfully and happily navigate life's challenges and live heroically. This book is another in a series of books dictated to Gina Lake by Jesus.

In the World but Not of It: New Teachings from Jesus on Embodying the Divine: From the Introduction, by Jesus: "What I have come to teach now is that you can embody love, as I did. You can learn to embody all that is good within you. I came to show you the beauty of your own soul and what is possible as a human. I came to show you that it is possible to be both human and divine, to be love incarnate. You walk with one foot in the world of form and another in the Formless. This mysterious duality within your being is what this book is about." This book is another in a series of books dictated to Gina Lake by Jesus.

All Grace: New Teachings from Jesus on the Truth About Life. Grace is the mysterious and unseen movement of God upon creation, which is motivated by love and indistinct from love. *All Grace* was given to Gina Lake by Jesus and represents his wisdom and understanding of life. It is about the magnificent and incomprehensible force behind life, which created life, sustains it, and operates within it as you and me and all of creation. *All Grace* is full of profound and life-changing truth.

Awakening Love: How to Love Your Neighbor as Yourself: "This book is what I would teach about love if I were walking among you today. It takes its organization from particular quotes of mine and others from the Bible, which have come down through time. The quotes this book is built upon are the core teachings I gave then and I offer you today. If they are adhered to, they will change your life and change your world." –Jesus

Faith, Facts, and Fiction: Finding Your Way on the Spiritual Path. In this channeled book by Jesus, he explains the ways people fool themselves and are fooled on the spiritual path and corrects many of the misunderstandings that many seekers have.

For more information, please visit the "Books" page at
www.RadicalHappiness.com

Made in the USA
Las Vegas, NV
31 October 2023

80053674R00142